ANCHORED
AND
INTENTIONAL

Sheila Wherry

ANCHORED
AND
INTENTIONAL

First published in Australia in 2025 by Sheila Wherry

Every effort has been made to trace and acknowledge all sources of
quotations and copyright material. Any unintentional omission will be
corrected in future editions, provided written notification is given to the
author.

This publication is intended for general information only and does not
constitute legal, health, or other professional advice. It is not intended to be
comprehensive or a substitute for such advice. You should seek professional
guidance, as appropriate, before acting on any of the content.

The client stories included in this book are composites drawn from real
coaching work. Names, sectors, and identifying details have been changed
to protect confidentiality, and any resemblance to actual persons is purely
coincidental.

ISBN 978-0-6488729-2-4
Cover design by Melanie Feddersen, i2i Design
Structural edit by Bernadette Foley, Broadcast Books
Copy edit by Marc McLean
Printed and distributed by IngramSpark

For more information, visit
www.eiexecutive.com.au

For my dear loved ones

CONTENTS

FOREWORD

Over the years, I've come to know Sheila through our work together – both in her capacity as an Executive Coach and a Leadership Team Coach. I've referred her to others and witnessed the growth they've experienced through working with her. My own experience reflects this – Sheila has helped me build an executive career anchored in people-first principles, all while navigating her own personal battles with courage, curiosity, and innate wisdom.

This book is inspiring. No doubt you'll find yourself reflecting on Sheila's compelling personal stories, professional coaching accounts, and the Stoic principles woven throughout – wherever you happen to find yourself on your leadership journey.

It's a book you can return to many times, with each reading revealing new insights. Personally, on my first read, the section on temperance was particularly thought-provoking. It emphasised the importance of leading with steadiness, even during a storm, as I navigated critical team and organisational changes.

A perfect balance of theory and practical wisdom drawn from real-life stories, this book is invaluable

– offering actionable insights and practical applications that make it not just a good read, but a guide for leadership and personal growth.

Thank you, Sheila, for this remarkable work. It's a beacon of wisdom and strength – one I know will guide many others as they explore what it means to lead with intention, grounded in what matters most.

Amalie Smith
Chief Operations, People & Safety Officer

Introduction

ANCHORED AND INTENTIONAL LEADERSHIP – WHY STOICISM, WHY NOW?

A few years ago, a close friend made an offhand comment that struck a chord: *'You approach life like a Stoic'.* The idea stayed with me – it planted a seed. I'd heard of the Stoics – Marcus Aurelius[1], Seneca[2], Epictetus[3] – but I hadn't studied them closely. I certainly didn't see myself reflected in ancient Roman philosophers. But as I began to read more, I recognised something deeply familiar – not just in their ideas, but in the way I had already been approaching life and leadership.

---

1   Marcus Aurelius – Roman Emperor and Stoic philosopher, best known for *Meditations,* his reflections on leadership, resilience, and ethical living.
2   Seneca – Roman statesman and Stoic philosopher, known for his letters on ethics, adversity, and self-mastery.
3   Epictetus – Former slave turned philosopher, known for teaching the power of personal choice and self-discipline.

Stoicism spoke to me in a way that was both grounding and galvanising. It offered a language for things I had long valued: intentionality, perspective, composure, and the ability to act with strength even when things are uncertain. It also made me realise that much of what I'd studied – psychotherapy, human behaviour, leadership theory and coaching – had already been captured by the Stoics in a way that was remarkably clear. Practical, usable, and grounded in the real world – that's what drew me in.

As an executive and team coach, I work with senior leaders across many sectors – people who hold immense responsibility and operate under relentless pressure. Some come to coaching feeling stuck or overwhelmed. Others are thriving and want to stay sharp and deliberate in how they lead. But regardless of where they start, the same questions tend to emerge – about leading themselves, and leading others.

- How do I keep my mindset strong when the pressure builds or doubt creeps in?
- How do I stay clear-headed when everything is moving fast?
- How do I navigate pressure without burning out – or becoming reactive?
- How do I support others with steadiness and care?
- How do I lead well when there are no easy answers?

This book was written to walk alongside you in those questions.

Whether you're in the thick of a leadership challenge or simply want to show up more intentionally for yourself and others, these are the kinds of questions that matter most. And that's what led me back to Stoicism – not as a theory, but as a practical lens to help navigate exactly these moments.

Offering Perspective, Not Rescue

This book isn't here to fix you. You don't need fixing. It's a companion to help you reflect, recalibrate, and lead from a place of steadiness – especially when the path ahead is complex or unclear.

You'll notice client stories throughout the book. They're included to offer recognition and resonance – so you can see yourself in the stories and know you're not alone in your experience. You may see yourself in these leaders – in their questions, their challenges, their growth. Each story is based on real conversations, shared with permission and adapted to protect confidentiality. I've included them because leadership can feel isolating, and recognising our shared humanity matters.

You'll also find some of my own story woven in. While I've spent years guiding others, I've also had moments of being brought to my knees – through sudden hearing loss and the kind of deep-seated struggles life can bring when you least expect them. And in the everyday moments too – the second-guessing, the mind chatter, the quiet weight of uncertainty.

Stoicism gives me, and many of the leaders I work with, something solid to stand on. Not certainty, but clarity. Not control, but courage. Not perfection, but presence.

That's what I want for you, too.

A Simple but Powerful Philosophy

Stoicism began over 2,000 years ago in ancient Greece. It was developed by philosophers[4] like Zeno, Cleanthes, and later, Roman thinkers such as Seneca (a statesman and advisor), Epictetus (a former slave turned teacher), and Marcus Aurelius (a Roman Emperor who ruled with both strength and introspection).

Their writings were not abstract theories. They were field notes for living well – especially in times of uncertainty, conflict, and pressure.

What's remarkable is how relevant their insights remain today. Despite the time and cultural distance, their reflections feel like they were written for modern leadership. They spoke of ambition, power, fear, loss, and the desire to live with meaning. They wrestled with the same things we do now.

The core ideas of Stoicism are simple – but not always easy to live.

They invite us to shift our focus from what we can't control to what we can: our perspective, our choices, and our character.

---

4   For an overview of early Stoic philosophers, see Diogenes Laertius, *Lives of Eminent Philosophers*, trans. R.D. Hicks (Loeb Classical Library, Harvard University Press, Cambridge, 1925), Book 7.

At its heart, Stoicism teaches us:

That life is short (*Memento Mori*) – so live with intention. That everything we face – good or bad – can shape us for the better (*Amor Fati*). That peace of mind begins when we let go of what's outside our control. And that what matters most isn't what happens – but how we choose to respond.

And guiding us along the way are four Stoic virtues – not lofty ideals, but practical, everyday commitments that help us lead well, especially under pressure.

The ability to pause, reflect, and see the bigger picture before you act: wisdom.

The willingness to show up and take action – even when the outcome isn't guaranteed, or when doubt and fear are close at hand: courage.

A commitment to doing what's right and fair – not just for ourselves, but in service of others, even when it's inconvenient or unseen: justice.

And the discipline to know when to speak and when to listen, when to push and when to step back: temperance.

These qualities are practical anchors we can hold onto. They steady us in uncertainty, and they keep us grounded in how we want to show up – every day, in every decision.

Who This Book Is For

Whether you're navigating deep challenges or simply want to lead with more strength and intention, this book offers tools and perspective to help you show up with purpose – especially when it matters most.

Each chapter explores one Stoic idea or practice, brought to life through client stories, coaching insights, and practical reflection. The first half focuses on the *inner world of leadership* – your mindset, your clarity, your presence. The second half focuses on the *outer world of leadership* and moves into action – how you make decisions, navigate difficulty, and lead others through complexity.

There's no need to read it all in one go. Take what you need. Reflect. Apply. Return.

Because Anchored and Intentional leadership isn't something you master once. It's something you practise daily.

Before we dive into the first principle, I want to start with a story. One that shows what anchored and intentional leadership can look like in real life.

Chapter 1

A LETTER FROM EXPERIENCE

When I first sat down to write this book, I thought about all the conversations I've had with senior leaders over the years. People at the top of their game – respected, successful, admired. Yet, when you listen closely, there's a common thread in their stories: the moment life cracked them open. The moment they realised the world wouldn't bend to their will. The moment they had to decide: Do I let this break me, or do I build myself anew? Or perhaps it wasn't one defining moment, but a series of life lessons – each one forcing them to dig deep, consider their choices, and build the discipline to consciously manage their mindset, actions, and intentions. This is Stoicism in action – the practice of meeting life as it is, taking responsibility for what's within our control – our choices and our actions.

One of my clients – I'll call her Kate – an executive leader, once shared her story with me. It stayed with me – not just because of what she went through, but because of what she took from it and how closely it aligned with Stoicism. I asked her if she'd be willing to share a part of it here. She agreed.

So, here it is – her experience, in her words.

'Everyone says I'm strong, that I just get on with things. But how did I get here? Was I born this way? I don't think so. Life changed for me when I lost my mum. It sent me to a dark place – one I wasn't sure I'd come out of. And yet, when I did, I saw the world differently. I realised how lucky I was. When you've been to the depths of grief, you don't just come back – you come back different. Stronger, yes. But also more grateful.

It's funny, though. I see people who appear to have had relatively easy lives – good family, no major losses – and yet they struggle to find that same sense of gratitude. They get caught in the *little* things, weighed down by problems that aren't truly problems. Maybe that's just human nature, or maybe it's what someone once called a "comfort crisis" – we have so much, but we struggle to appreciate it.

For me, work has been a proving ground. You deal with so many people – different backgrounds, different perspectives. It's easy to judge, to expect people to toughen up, to just *get on with it*. But I've learned that real leadership means seeing beyond the surface. It means empathy, understanding that some people are carrying things you'll never fully grasp. And that doesn't mean you lower the bar. It means you lead differently. You listen more. You engage more. You bring people along rather than dragging them forward.

Through all of this, I've learned to let go of things that don't serve me. Other people's opinions? If they don't influence what I'm trying to achieve, why should they hold power over me? I live by my values, and I've come to see that the Stoic virtues – wisdom, courage, justice, and temperance – align closely with the way I've always tried to lead. I used to worry about being liked. Now, I focus on being respected – for my consistency, for my fairness, for my ability to make tough calls without losing my humanity.

But at the core of it all, I've realised something simple: To be truly strong, you have to be grateful first. And not just the kind of gratitude where you write down three good things before bed—though that helps. I mean real gratitude. The kind that acknowledges both the joy and the suffering. The kind that looks at hardship and says, "I wouldn't want to go through that again, but I wouldn't trade what I learned from it either."

Life is finite. One day, I won't be here. In a hundred years, no one will remember me. And that's not a depressing thought. It's a freeing one. Because if that's the case, then I'd better make the most of the time I do have. I'd better spend it wisely. I'd better live fully. Because what a waste otherwise.'

I wanted to start this book with her words because they capture the heart of what follows. This isn't a book about leadership in the traditional sense – about strategy, metrics, or performance. It's about something deeper. It's about what anchors you when life inevitably shakes you. It's about what keeps you intentional when the easy path calls. It's about mindset and action.

As you move through this book, you may start to recognise just how many Stoic principles are woven into her story – how she wasn't talking Stoicism, she was living it. She applied it in real time to navigate life's hardest moments, shape her daily choices and interactions, and define her path forward.

You have the power to choose – how you see the world, how you respond to adversity, and how you use the time you've been given. This truth sits at the heart of everything in these pages.

The Choice We All Face

You've already heard one leader's story – a personal account of adversity, strength, and the power of perspective. Her experience illustrates something fundamental: life doesn't offer certainty, but it does offer choices.

As a senior leader, you navigate complexity every day. You don't just manage teams and strategies – you manage yourself. Your mindset. Your energy. Your response to the unexpected. And in that constant navigation, you face a choice: do you resist what you can't control, or do you anchor yourself in what you can?

The best leaders I've worked with don't waste energy fighting the uncontrollable. Instead, they focus on themselves – their thoughts, actions, and behaviours. They train their minds to stay clear and grounded, and they think deliberately about how they act.

The Reality of Leadership

The world will always be unpredictable. Teams will change. Conditions will shift. Crises will arise. Through it all, the most effective leaders remain anchored and intentional.

Leadership is deeply human work. It requires genuine inner strength – the kind that's built slowly and steadily through self-awareness, challenges, and lived experience – not a surface-level show of confidence or control that's just for appearances. It takes self-awareness to notice when you're caught in frustration or resistance, and discipline to shift your focus toward what actually matters: cultivating an anchored mindset.

Anchored leaders centre themselves in what they can influence. They bring clarity of thought. They stay present, even when the path ahead is uncertain. They take intentional action.

Applying Stoicism:
A PRACTICAL PATH FORWARD

The ancient Stoics deeply understood this. They didn't preach detachment from reality; they practiced engagement with it – fully, intentionally, and with clear purpose. They trained their minds to withstand setbacks, to embrace change, and to act with courage.

That's why this book draws on Stoic principles – not as an abstract philosophy, but as a practical framework for leadership and life. These tools and perspectives are offered to help you manage your mindset, regulate emotions, and make better decisions – so that when challenges arise, you don't react impulsively. You respond with clarity.

I've had to walk this path myself. I know what it's like to feel the ground has been pulled from under you, to face moments that force you to rethink everything. I'm not here to tell you that Stoicism is *the* answer. But I am here to share what I've learned, what has helped me, and what I've seen support my clients.

For me, Stoicism became more than something I had read about – it became something I *had* to put into practice. Like anyone faced with adversity, I didn't get to choose whether to go through it. I only got to choose how.

Here's how that happened…

Living with Uncertainty:
A PERSONAL STORY

It started suddenly. One afternoon in November 2023, after playing a game of padel (a combination of tennis and squash, and highly addictive!), I went for a drink with friends. I sat at the end of a long table, struggling to hear conversations. It felt strange – like one side of the world had gone silent. I assumed it was an ear infection. When I got home, I shared with my family, 'Something's not right with my ear.'

The next morning, I went to the doctor. 'Nothing wrong,' was the verdict. A few days later, another doctor: 'Maybe an infection,' he suggested. The prescribed medication did nothing. But I knew. This wasn't normal. My hearing felt distant, warped – like I was underwater. I started hearing unusual sounds: water running, clicking, ringing.

On the third visit to the A&E that week, I finally saw an Ear, Nose and Throat (ENT) Registrar who recognised what was happening. 'This is sudden sensorineural hearing loss – SSNHL. It's a medical emergency.' An audiology test confirmed I had sudden and profound hearing loss in my right ear.

I started on high-dose steroids, which didn't work – nor did the three steroid injections, into my inner ear, that followed. They were more likely to help if treatment had started in the first 24-48 hours. But ten days had already passed, and by then, it was anyone's guess.

The doctors had no explanation as to what caused it. 'Possibly a virus, or a bacterial infection,' they said.

'Or it could be autoimmune, which opens the possibility of losing the hearing in the other ear. There's no way to know.' And they couldn't tell me if my hearing would return.

And so, I waited. I lived with uncertainty.

From my partner's perspective, it was horrific to watch. The fear started to settle in – not just for me, but for those around me. The noise sensitivity was intense – everyday sounds, like a fork hitting the counter or a tap running, felt like an assault. Voices at the wrong pitch could trigger pain. The tinnitus was relentless, my brain's way of filling the silence where sound used to be.

I started withdrawing. It felt like the only way to cope. Google became my refuge – searching for answers, grasping at anything that might explain what had happened or offer a way forward.

But there were no answers. Only silence. And uncertainty.

The grief of losing my hearing overnight was overwhelming. I felt like I was losing parts of myself – my social life, my confidence.

Depression tried to creep in. My partner could see it happening, but didn't know how to help. And in trying not to burden me, they withdrew too. We were both lost in different ways.

At my three-month check-up, the ENT confirmed it would take a miracle for my hearing to come back. 'Many learn to live with single-sided deafness,' he remarked.

I found that unacceptable.

I wanted my life back – the ability to fully engage in conversations, to laugh with my family and friends, to feel present, to navigate the world without lip reading and constant exhaustion. But I had no certainty. No clear path forward.

That was when I asked myself the question that would shift everything: Who do I want to be in the face of this adversity?

I had no control over what had happened – but what could I control? How could I shift my thinking? How could I keep moving forward when I had no guarantees? How did I want to experience myself – and how did I want others to experience me?

I threw myself into research. I met with specialists. I toured a cochlear implant facility. My focus shifted from grief to action. My partner saw it happen – one day, something clicked, and I was back. Not fully, not yet. But there was a spark. A determination. A sense of agency.

By the time I returned to my ENT at the six-month mark, I walked in and said, 'I want to move forward with a cochlear implant.' I had done the work. I understood the risks and the next steps. I had a team lined up. I even had a date in mind. He nodded in support, opened his calendar, and booked me in.

The surgery was daunting. Actually, that's an understatement – I was absolutely terrified. They drilled through my skull and inserted an electrode into my inner ear. The implant didn't restore natural hearing – it was something else entirely. I had to retrain my brain to interpret sound. At first, voices were a series of beeps. Then they sounded robotic. Over time, through disciplined rehab, I started to make sense of speech again.

The experience changed me. Profoundly.

I already knew the importance of connection through my work. But that awareness became magnified during this period. My family and friends, my clients, the care of my medical team, my fellow padel players – they were a lifeline.

One of the most unexpected shifts was in my relationship with strength – both mental and physical. This experience taught me that I am stronger, mentally, than I ever knew.

I started strength training more seriously and single-mindedly than I ever had. I wanted to cultivate ongoing grit – not just in my mindset, but in my body. Voluntary discomfort became a practice: choosing to do something hard every day (in the form of exercise), so that when life throws another challenge my way, I'll be ready. I'll have trained for it.

Because life will throw challenges my way.

This experience reinforced what I had always believed: we don't control what happens to us, but we do control how we respond.

Chapter 2

WHEN (STOIC) THEORY BECOMES (LEADERSHIP) PRACTICE

I've always been fascinated by the moments that redefine us – the unexpected challenges that force us to see the world, and ourselves, in an entirely new way. Mine came overnight. One moment, I could hear. The next…silence.

I'd read about Stoicism. I'd even shared its principles with my clients. But when certainty disappeared, theory wasn't enough. I had to live it. Stoicism became my daily guide – not just a philosophy, but a survival mindset. It shaped my choices and helped me navigate the unknown.

As I began sharing these principles more intentionally in coaching, I noticed something interesting: some clients were already using Stoic ideas without realising it. Others, when introduced to them, instantly recognised their power. It struck me that in a world overflowing with complex leadership frameworks, the essence of human grit, decision-making, and focus had been distilled over two thousand years ago. Business books offer new models, but the core challenges of leadership remain the same: how to lead ourselves and others with clarity, respond with sound judgment, and act with intention.

That's why I wrote this book.

Anchored and Intentional offers a grounded, flexible approach to leadership. It's an invitation – to reflect, to consider, and to apply what resonates. That act of choosing – of engaging thoughtfully and adapting with purpose – is a Stoic practice in itself.

I use these principles quietly in the background of coaching conversations – drawing on them when they help a leader think clearly, stay steady, or move through something difficult. Sometimes I name the idea. Often, I don't. What matters is the conversation we're in: what the leader is wrestling with, what they're trying to hold steady through, and what kind of leader they want to be.

This book follows that same spirit. The principles are here to support you – whether you're looking for fresh perspective, practical tools, or a steadying mindset during challenging times. You'll find ideas you can work with right away, and others that may take root over time.

Each chapter explores one Stoic idea or practice, brought to life through client stories, coaching insights, and practical reflection. You might connect deeply with one chapter and return to another when the moment calls for it. There's no need to absorb it all at once.

Let this be a companion – something you can return to, again and again, as you show up in your role, reflect on what matters, and take your next step.

HOW THE BOOK IS SHAPED

This book is divided into three parts.

Part 1: Anchored Mindset

Anchored leadership begins with mindset – your ability to stay steady in uncertainty. Life is unpredictable. The pace of change can feel relentless. Anchored leadership helps you navigate this by staying grounded in what's within your control. It supports clear thinking and emotional steadiness. It's about meeting the moment with perspective, presence, and appreciation for what is.

Part 2: Intentional Action

Intentional leadership is about how you act – choosing your responses with clarity and confidence. It means standing firm in hard decisions, leading with fairness, and maintaining balance under pressure. Intentional leadership helps you move forward with conviction, even when the way ahead is unclear. It's knowing when to act decisively, and when to pause and adapt with purpose.

Part 3: Staying On Track – Weekly Reflections For Leadership Practice

Finally, the third part of the book offers reflections for staying on track – 52 weekly prompts that pair a Stoic idea with a question to consider and a real-life coaching story to help you pause, reflect, and reset.

This book is written with senior leaders in mind – drawing from real coaching conversations and lived experiences at the executive level – but the ideas are universal. Whether you lead a team or contribute as an individual, leadership today asks all of us to take responsibility for how we show up, support each other, and navigate challenges.

Leadership is rooted in presence, mindset, and intentional action. This book offers timeless principles, practical insights, and space for reflection to support you in that work. Take what feels most relevant right now, and return to the rest when the moment calls for it.

By engaging with this book on your terms, you're already practising Stoicism. And in that space – of choice, reflection, and intention – is where real leadership begins.

PART 1

Anchored Mindset

This first section of the book focuses on your inner world – the mindset and mental discipline that support everything else you do as a leader.

Anchored leadership means staying steady in uncertainty – recognising what's within your control, and letting go of what isn't. The focus is on strengthening your capacity to think clearly, make reasoned choices, and maintain emotional steadiness. It's an invitation to appreciate what is, rather than fight what isn't.

We don't rise to every moment of chaos and challenge with perfect composure. But we can practise. And we can prepare.

What's Next?

One of the most powerful ways we take control of our response to life is by recognising its brevity. We don't have forever. And that truth changes everything.

In the next chapter, we explore *Memento Mori* – the Stoic practice of remembering that life is finite. Not as a morbid thought, but as a clarifying one. Because when we accept life's impermanence, we stop wasting it. We stop delaying what matters. And we start leading – and living – with greater intention.

Chapter 3

THE ONE CERTAINTY – MEMENTO MORI

'Let us prepare our minds as if we'd come to the very end of life. Let us postpone nothing. Let us balance life's books each day. … The one who puts the finishing touches on their life each day is never short of time.'

– SENECA[5]

Have you ever had a moment where life suddenly felt fragile? Where you realised – not intellectually, but deep in your bones – that time is running out?

Perhaps it was the loss of someone close to you. A sudden health scare. A near-miss accident. Or maybe it was something quieter – a sentence in a book, a conversation with a friend, an ordinary moment that suddenly made you realise just how little control you have over time.

---

5   Seneca, *Letters to Lucilius*, Letter 101, public domain.

We like to believe we have time. That we will get to the important things later. That we can afford to wait.

But can we?

As an Executive and Leadership Team Coach, I work hard to remain curious, open to new ideas and perspectives. Yet, there's one truth I hold with unwavering certainty. The only certainty. We are all going to die. No exceptions.

And yet, many of us push this to the back of our minds. We delay important actions or conversations until the 'right time.' We put off difficult decisions, believing that there will be a more convenient moment down the line. We structure our lives as if time is something we have an unlimited supply of.

The Stoic principle of *Memento Mori – remember you must die –* is a clear-eyed reminder that life is finite. While the exact phrase doesn't appear in early Stoic texts, the concept was central to their thinking. Roman generals were said to have had it whispered in their ear during victory parades, as a way to stay grounded. For philosophers like Seneca, Epictetus, and Marcus Aurelius, it wasn't a gloomy statement – it was a daily practice that sharpened focus, stripped away distraction, and clarified what really matters. It called them – and it calls us – to live with urgency, presence, and intention.

Memento Mori isn't meant to be morbid. It's meant to wake us up. To pull us out of distraction. To help us focus on what truly matters.

Steve Jobs, co-founder of Apple, captured this when he told a graduating class at Stanford:

'Remembering that you are going to die is the best way I know to avoid the trap of thinking you have something to lose. Your time is limited, so don't waste it living someone else's life.'[6]

So, the question is: Are you living your life, or are you simply moving through it, assuming you'll always have more time?

Stop Delaying

It's easy to tell ourselves we'll get to the important things later.

Later, we'll focus on our health. Later, we'll spend more time with the people we care about. Later, we'll make the changes we know we need to make.

But what if later never comes?

It's tempting to think in terms of years – where do I want to be in five years? But the truth is, we don't know how much time we have. *Memento Mori* shifts our focus to now.

Rather than getting caught up in an uncertain future, this mindset brings us back to the present. It prompts us to consider the choices we're making today, what we're prioritising, and where we might be wasting time. This isn't about abandoning responsibility or making reckless decisions – it's about being deliberate.

---

6   Steve Jobs, *Stanford Commencement Address*, Stanford University, June 12, 2005. Available at: https://news.stanford.edu/2005/06/14/jobs-061505/

When we assume we have unlimited time, we become complacent. We put off hard conversations. We avoid risks. We tell ourselves we'll act when the conditions are perfect.

But there is no perfect moment.

The more we assume we have time, the more we lose our sense of urgency.

The more we remember it's finite, the more we live with intention.

What Truly Matters

Have you ever noticed how certain worries seem urgent in the moment but, when you step back, they fade into the background?

Frustrations that once felt consuming – an email that irritated you, a meeting that didn't go well – often lose their weight when viewed from a distance.

If you were to zoom out on your life right now, what would still matter?

Mo Gawdat, a former Google executive and author of *Solve for Happy*[7], speaks about life as a rental. We don't own it. We are merely borrowing time, and one day, we will have to give it back.

It's a simple idea. But living it? Not always easy.

There was a moment in my own career when I had to ask myself some hard questions – the kind I now hear echoed by so many of my clients.

---

7   M Gawdat, *Solve for Happy: Engineer Your Path to Joy*, Bluebird, London, 2017, Chapter 5.

At the time, I was working for a Swedish healthcare company, responsible for building their business across Southeast Asia. We made virtual reality surgical simulators – technology that gave surgeons the chance to practise and refine their skills in a simulated environment, rather than on real patients. It was meaningful work, and I felt proud to be part of something that was genuinely improving people's lives.

The role was dynamic and global. Every month, I was travelling across Asia, often away for a week at a time. I loved the energy – the mix of cultures, the relationships I was building, the challenge of growing something from the ground up. For a season, it was exactly where I wanted to be.

Then I had a baby. And everything shifted.

The travel lost its appeal. More than that, I found myself longing to be more present – not just at home, but in my conversations, in my work, in my life. I wanted to connect with others in a deeper, more human way. I wanted to understand what made people tick, and how we could lead and live with more intention and meaning.

So I made the decision to resign.

It was a leap into the unknown. I didn't have a clear plan. But I knew what I valued – my son, my time, and my own growth. I returned to study, completing a Masters in Management, followed by postgraduate qualifications in counselling, psychotherapy, and executive coaching.

I couldn't yet see where it would all lead. But I trusted the direction. I wanted a career that lit me up – work that felt aligned, purposeful, and deeply human. And I've never regretted it. That time with my son during his early years built a bond that still holds strong today – he's now 20. And I've built an executive coaching business that energises and fulfils me every day.

This story often resonates with the senior leaders I now work with. Not because they all want to step away – but because they recognise the moment. The moment when you realise you *do* have a choice. When you stop chasing someone else's version of success and start listening to what really matters. When you ask: 'Who do I choose to be now? What gives me energy? What's truly important?'

Answer those questions, and everything shifts.

It takes courage to make those choices. But *Memento Mori* is a quiet reminder: we don't have forever.

Leading Like Time Is Finite

If time is finite, how does that change the way you show up as a leader? Does it shift how you handle conflict, what you give your attention to, or how you engage with your team?

We often think about leadership in terms of long-term impact. But the best leaders understand that influence is not built in years – it is built in moments. Every conversation, every decision, every action is a vote for the kind of leader you are becoming.

James Clear, author of *Atomic Habits*[8], puts it simply: 'Every action you take is a vote for the type

---

8   J Clear, *Atomic Habits: An Easy & Proven Way to Build Good Habits & Break Bad Ones*, Penguin Random House, New York, 2018.

of person you wish to become.' The same holds true in leadership.

How you handle conflict isn't about one big decision – it's shaped by the small moments where you choose to listen before reacting. What you give your attention to isn't determined by your calendar – it's revealed in the way you show up for your team, even when you're busy. How you engage with others isn't just about your leadership philosophy – it's built through every conversation.

So rather than focusing only on who you want to be in five years, ask yourself: Who am I choosing to be today?

Leadership is about both – what you achieve and how you show up, moment by moment.

Closing Reflection:
THE ONE CERTAINTY

Seneca wrote: 'Death is not an evil. What is it then? The one law mankind has that is free of all discrimination.'[9]

Memento Mori is not about fear. It is about freedom.

It strips away the unnecessary.

It sharpens focus.

It reminds us that now – not later – is the time to act with intention, to make choices that align with who we want to be and the impact we want to have.

---

9   Seneca, *Moral Letters to Lucilius*, trans. R M Gummere,
Loeb Classical Library, Harvard University Press, Cambridge, 1917,
Letter 30, public domain; adapted by the author.

This isn't a concept you check off on a list. It is something you carry with you.

And as you continue through this book, you'll see how it shapes everything else – your mindset, your actions, and ultimately, the way you live.

Because when you truly accept that life is short, you stop wasting it on things that don't align with who you want to be.

Finding Yourself Beyond Work –
A MEMENTO MORI REFLECTION

Leila, a senior leader navigating change, shared with me the moment she truly understood the meaning of *Memento Mori – remember you must die –* and how it gave her the courage to make tough decisions, and the willingness to do the deep introspection she hadn't allowed herself the time or space for until then.

She had spent years in a demanding leadership role. As a Deputy Director in a large public institution, her days were full – strategic meetings, tight timelines, and the constant juggle of delivering results while supporting a team. Eventually, she made the bold move into a new position as Executive Director of a mission-driven organisation delivering international programs. But the biggest shift wasn't the job. It was what happened in between.

'Memento Mori became real for me the moment I acknowledged a simple truth: life is short. I wasn't happy in my role or organisation, and I had been putting off making a change. I kept telling myself there would be time to figure things out, time to prioritise myself later. But when I finally let myself sit with the truth – that time isn't guaranteed – I knew I had to stop waiting.'

She made the call to step away.

'At first, it was terrifying. Work had always given me direction, purpose, and a clear sense of who I was. And I had worked extremely hard to get there. Without it, I felt at sea, completely unanchored. I questioned everything. Am I good enough? Who am I without my work identity? What next? What do I actually want?'

As we talked, I could hear how much she had held – how much responsibility, care, and striving had shaped her professional life. What struck me was her honesty, especially as she described what it meant to stop and truly sit with the big questions.

'I had spent years pouring myself into my career, balancing work, ageing parents, and kids – making sure everything and everyone was taken care of. But I had never truly taken the time to stop and ask: What do I want? What makes me happy?'

She admitted that her first instinct was to fill the space with activity.

'Initially, I filled my time with big projects – because that's what I knew. I was so used to having goals, moving forward, proving my worth through achievement. But then I realised – I was doing the exact same thing again. I had stepped away from work, yet I was still trying to measure myself through productivity.

So I stopped.'

That pause changed everything. Not overnight, but gradually – through reflection, questioning, and sitting with the discomfort of not having all the answers.

'I sat still, reflected, and delved deeper into myself. What do I actually *want? What brings me joy?'*

She spoke about how much of her identity had been tied to performance, to being seen as capable, liked, and effective.

'I came to see that I had always sought external validation – measuring my worth through how well I and my team performed, how others saw me, and the results I produced. My value had been tied to success, being liked, and constantly proving myself.

I told myself: You have the self-agency to change your thinking, and to answer the hard questions you're sitting with.'

What moved her forward was the realisation that she wasn't alone in this experience.

'There were so many other capable, smart women who had spent their whole lives looking after

careers, children, ageing parents – caught in the constant motion of responsibility. Women who, like me, had been so focused on doing everything right that they had never paused to think about what they actually wanted for themselves with the finite time they have.

Seeing this gave me a sense of comfort. I wasn't failing. I wasn't lost. I was simply asking the right questions for the first time.'

She didn't gloss over the difficulty. Letting go of control and sitting in uncertainty was hard – and unfamiliar.

'At first, sitting in the uncertainty felt overwhelming. I had always been someone who sought control – knowing what's happening, planning, structuring, organising. But this experience forced me to let go. To be okay without it. To even find humour in chaos.'

But in that space, she began to clarify what mattered most.

'As I sat, reflected, and went deeper into understanding what I truly wanted, clarity came.

With this, I refined what I wanted for myself, professionally and personally. I found a new role – not just any job, but one that felt purposeful and meaningful. One that aligned with my values and made me feel like I was contributing something that mattered.'

And with that came a shift – not just in work, but in how she now lives her life.

'Today, I experience my life differently. This period has taught me to sit in the grey, and now I'm so much better at it. I've found joy, perspective, and a deeper understanding of myself. And all of it started with one simple, but profound, thought: Life is short. I need to live now.'

Reflective Questions

These questions aren't about having all the answers – they're an invitation to pause, check in with yourself, and notice what matters most.

- What am I putting off, waiting for the 'right time'?
- What truly matters to me – beyond titles, roles, or other people's expectations?
- If I was to act with the knowledge that time is finite, what decision would I make today?
- Where in my life am I filling space with activity rather than intention?
- What would it look like to live more fully now – not later?

When you're ready, we'll build on this in the next chapter.

What's Next?

Building on this foundation, the next chapter will explore the Stoic principle of *Amor Fati*, which challenges us to embrace and love everything that life brings – whether it's good, bad, or somewhere in between.

Chapter 4

EMBRACE IT ALL – AMOR FATI

*'Love the hand that fate deals you and play it
as your own, for what could be more fitting?'*

– MARCUS AURELIUS[10]

There are moments in life when everything shifts in an instant.

A conversation you weren't expecting. A decision made without your input. A personal loss that leaves you breathless. One moment, you think you know where you're heading; the next, the path disappears.

In those moments, it's easy to resist – to wish things had gone differently. But what if, instead of fighting against what is, you leaned into it?

The same is true in leadership. A lost deal. A failed project. A difficult team member. The unexpected

---

10   M Aurelius, *Meditations*, adapted from the public domain translation by G Long, 1862, Book 6, Section 30.

will come. The question isn't *if* you will face challenge and adversity – it's *how* you will meet it.

What if, instead of resisting and wrestling with these challenges, you embraced them? What if you saw every experience – both positive and difficult – as necessary and beneficial?

This mindset doesn't call for gritting your teeth through hardship or pretending everything is okay. It asks you to actively lean into what life brings, believing that every event is shaping you in the way it needs to.

The most grounded leaders I work with aren't the ones who avoid challenge; they're the ones who walk towards it, knowing that growth doesn't come from ease – it comes from how we respond to what we cannot control.

They adopt an active mindset shift: *This happened for me. Not to me.*

That's not easy. Especially when life presents profound difficulty. And yet, those who take this approach often find that these moments – however painful – become the greatest learning opportunities of their lives.

Learning to Embrace What Is

When something difficult happens, Stoicism encourages us to ask:

- *What is this teaching me?*
- *What can I learn from this?*

Life continually sends us back to school. Every experience gives us the chance to reconsider our perspectives, to expand how we think, feel, and act in the world. To refine how we lead. To uncover strengths we didn't know we had. To face our blind spots and choose how we want to address them.

Amor Fati doesn't ask us to merely tolerate life's difficulties – it asks us to actively love them.

To stop seeing challenges as interruptions and start seeing them as part of the path.

It's a choice.

You can embrace what happens to you and find meaning in it, or you can fight it. You can argue with reality, resist change, and struggle against what is. But life has a way of continuing on, whether we fight it or not.

So why not develop the capacity to truly love it all – the expected and the unexpected, the easy and the impossible?

That's where freedom is found. Not in changing what happens, but in changing how you meet it.

A Lesson in Acceptance

The idea of embracing what life brings came into sharp focus one afternoon when my phone buzzed. A message from my client, Blake: 'Can you talk?'

It was unusual for him to reach out like that, and I sensed something significant was weighing on his mind. When I called back, the silence on the other end of the line was palpable. After a moment, Blake spoke, his voice heavy with emotion.

He had just been made redundant – his position eliminated in the latest wave of organisational restructuring. After years of dedication to his role – leading a team through change, delivering significant results – it was over. Worst of all, he was blindsided.

For years, Blake had been building something he was proud of. His team had thrived under his leadership. His division had delivered outstanding results. He had assumed his career trajectory was solid. And then, in a single meeting, it was gone. 'It feels like everything I've built doesn't matter anymore', he declared. 'My team, our work – it's like it all vanished in an instant.'

His reaction was deeply human. The redundancy wasn't just a professional setback – it was personal. He wasn't only mourning the loss of a job; he was grieving an imagined future. And like many of us, he was wrestling not only with the event itself, but with the gap between what he expected and what had actually happened.

As we spoke, I reminded him that his pain was real. Losing a role – especially one so deeply tied to identity – can be profoundly destabilising. And yet, much of our suffering in these moments doesn't come from the loss alone – it comes from our resistance to it.

We cling to the *should-haves* and *what-ifs*, creating a space between reality and expectation. And it's in that space that suffering often sits. Acceptance, hard as it is, begins when we stop wrestling with what we can't change and start meeting what *is*.

But acceptance is not resignation. It's not about giving up. It's about turning to meet the moment – without judgment or resistance – and asking, *what now?*

Blake took a deep breath, and shared his realisation: 'I have a choice. I can let this define me, or I can use it.'

That was the shift – as he reflected later: 'Redundancy doesn't erase the skills I've built, the relationships I've fostered, or the value I bring. This is an opportunity to redefine my path – to build something that aligns with where I am now.'

He didn't pretend it wasn't painful. But he stopped resisting it. And that allowed him to move forward.

A Different Kind of Strength

Years ago, I taught a subject on grief and loss at a psychology college.

One of my students, Martha, shared privately that she had a progressive, terminal disease. As if that weren't heartbreaking enough, her young daughter carried the gene for the same condition.

Teaching a class on bereavement with Martha in the room was one of the hardest things I have ever done. She never asked for special treatment. She simply, and bravely, wanted to keep learning.

In class, we had many discussions about the meaning of life. She questioned whether suffering had meaning at all – and whether it needed to.

Later, she was invited to take part in a clinical trial for a potential treatment – one that could help not only her, but possibly her daughter too. She wrote to me, reflecting that maybe there was something to all those conversations we'd had about meaning. For the first time, it felt tangible. Taking part in that trial gave her something to hold on to – a sense that she could contribute to something bigger, something that might help her daughter and others down the track.

She saw herself as fortunate. Despite her prognosis, she held a quiet belief that things would unfold as they were meant to. It wasn't resignation – it was grace. She couldn't control what was happening to her, but she chose how she met it.

She embraced her fate with courage, love, and a deep sense of contribution.

As Viktor Frankl, a Holocaust survivor and psychiatrist, reminds us: 'If there is a meaning in life at all, then there must be a meaning in suffering.'[11]

Closing Reflection:
WELCOME IT ALL

Blake. Martha. The Stoics.

They all show us that true strength isn't about control – it's about trust.

Leaders who live by Amor Fati don't just tolerate adversity; they welcome it. They understand that every

---

11   Viktor E. Frankl, *Man's Search for Meaning: An Introduction to Logotherapy*, trans. Ilse Lasch, Washington Square Press, New York, 1963, p. 113.

challenge, every setback, every success is part of their path – shaping them day by day.

The invitation is not to keep wishing things were different.

It's to ask: 'How can I use this?'

Because when you embrace all of it – without resistance, without regret – you move beyond frustration and fear. You become open to whatever life brings next.

And that is where real leadership begins.

AMOR FATI IN ACTION

Charlie is a senior executive and a current coaching client. Over the course of our work together, we've had many rich conversations about Stoicism – how it applies to real leadership challenges, and how it offers something steady to hold onto when the ground underneath feels uncertain.

When I asked if he'd be open to sharing his reflections for this book, he generously agreed. Charlie didn't set out to be a Stoic leader – but he's become one, through intention, practice, and lived experience.

His story brings *Amor Fati* to life – not just as a Stoic phrase, but as a daily practice: the act of embracing life, exactly as it comes.

'I came across Stoicism about ten years ago. At first, I was reading out of pure interest, but the

more I explored, the more this philosophy (along with Buddhism) resonated with me – especially the ancient texts from philosophers like Marcus Aurelius, Epictetus, and Seneca. I was struck by how their wisdom, written thousands of years ago, is still so relevant to modern leadership challenges and my personal life.

As I read more, I realised that applying Stoic principles intentionally – rather than just understanding them intellectually – was where real growth happened. I began focusing on how Stoicism could help me develop as a leader and as a person.'

This idea of moving from intellectual understanding to embodied practice is something I see again and again in my work. For leaders, the real transformation doesn't come from reading the right book. It comes from asking: How will I apply this when the pressure is on? When things don't go my way? When I feel like quitting?

'One of the most profound lessons Stoicism has taught me is the importance of accepting reality – even the most difficult aspects of it. Wisdom isn't just about knowledge; it's about clarity. For me, Stoicism helped crystallise my sense of purpose – both in my career and personal life. It shaped how I make decisions, how I prioritise my family, and how I navigate uncertainty.

At the core of it all is the understanding that one day, I will take my final breath. I can't change the past, and I can't predict the future. The only thing I can control is how I show up in this moment. Time is finite. So, I ask myself daily: What am I doing? Why am I doing it? And how am I making the most of this present moment?'

When Charlie said this, I paused. This is what anchored the whole conversation: *Amor Fati* isn't about blind positivity. It's about seeing things clearly – and still choosing to engage with courage. It's the kind of courage that lets us face what's real, without shutting down or turning away.

'I often reflect on Memento Mori – the Stoic practice of remembering that life is short. It reminds me that I don't have time to waste. In my role, I have a responsibility to make a difference, and that starts with being fully present.

For me, that means giving people my full attention and truly listening. I recognise the power of words. Life is too short for excuses, self-pity, or waiting for the perfect moment. Instead, I focus on showing up, taking action, and doing my best – knowing that failure is part of the journey. Because failure is human.'

This is a beautiful example of grounded leadership. Choosing presence over perfection. What Charlie is doing here is simple, but not easy. And it's deeply Stoic.

'Ryan Holiday's The Obstacle Is the Way[12] reinforced something I had already started practising: using setbacks as signposts. Marcus Aurelius captured it best: "The obstacle to action becomes part of the action. What stands in the way becomes the way."[13]

I've experienced this firsthand. It's easy to feel frustrated by unfair systems or decisions. But Stoicism reminds me that when something blocks your path, you have a choice: see yourself as a victim, or ask, how can I grow from this?

Epictetus reminds us that no one but ourselves is responsible for our own judgments. This was a game-changer for me. In my early – even middle – career, I spent too much time worrying about what others thought of me, letting imagined fears cloud my decision-making. I let outside opinions shape my confidence. Over time, I realised that the only thing I truly control is my response – how I think, feel, and act.'

So often, I witness leaders get caught up in what others think – and they start to second guess themselves. Taking back that headspace is freeing. It's also part of being a responsible leader. Stoicism asks: 'Who's running your mind?' Charlie's answer is clear.

---

12   Ryan Holiday, *The Obstacle Is the Way: The Timeless Art of Turning Trials into Triumph* (New York: Portfolio, 2014). Holiday is a modern author and media strategist known for popularising Stoic philosophy.
13   M Aurelius, *Meditations*, trans. G Long, 1862, public domain; adapted by the author.

'In leadership, how we judge people and situations matters. It's not the events themselves that trouble us, but our judgments of them. If someone provokes us, our response is what defines us.

Now, my instinct is to pause – breathe – calm my mind before reacting. I've learned to stop wasting energy on things outside my control and focus on where I can have an impact. Energy can be scattered or directed. I choose to direct it.

Only I control my mind. I won't give that control away.'

In our coaching conversations, I experience Charlie as a remarkably intentional leader. He doesn't react – he reflects, then responds with clarity and calm. He is regularly faced with emotionally charged situations, and we often talk through his initial emotional reaction. Yet, what stands out is how he meets those moments: stepping back, seeing clearly, and choosing his response. This is what emotional control looks like from the inside out.

'Practising Stoicism isn't about having all the answers – it's about committing to small, daily habits that reinforce strength of mind. For me, journalling has been powerful. It helps me process emotions, clarify my thinking, and recognise where I haven't been at my best. It keeps me grounded.'

It's easy to overlook the power of small practices. But these are the habits that build the muscle of Stoicism over time. Rather than attempting to build a steady base once the storm has hit, Charlie's commitment to reflection and journalling has helped him lay the foundation early – so he can keep showing up clear-headed and steady when things get tough.

> 'One of my biggest leadership challenges came when I was appointed to a national chief role. I was tasked with merging departments, but beneath the surface was a hidden agenda – headcount reductions that weren't being communicated transparently.
>
> I created an organisational design strategy, but when I presented it, I was blindsided. Senior leaders told me it wouldn't meet their targets. I felt dejected. They didn't seem to understand the reality I was working with, and their expectations felt impossible.
>
> I considered walking away. I gave myself 24-48 hours to feel the frustration. And then I reminded myself: this is an opportunity, not just a roadblock. Instead of blaming others or retreating, I asked: "How do I lead through this while staying true to my values?"
>
> My purpose was clear – the organisation served vulnerable people. My loyalty was to that mission, and to my team. I processed the emotion but didn't let it dictate my actions.'

This was a moment of real leadership; when your values and your reality collide. Charlie's ability to feel the emotion, reflect, and then act from principle is a real example of Stoicism in practice. He explained:

'After journalling and reflecting, I approached things differently:

- *I asked direct questions to fully understand the senior leadership team's objectives.*
- *I reframed constraints as organisational design challenges.*
- *I brought my team in, openly sharing the uncertainty, and we tackled it together.*

Initially, it felt like a punch to the gut. But stepping back, I saw it wasn't personal. My ego had been bruised – but the bigger picture mattered more.

That experience shaped how I lead today. In my current role, I approach challenges with more certainty – not because the path is easier, but because I've trained myself to navigate it differently.

For example, when preparing for a high-stakes board meeting, my old mindset would have been filled with assumptions – imagining how the board would react, anticipating resistance, and letting those expectations shape my behaviour. Now, I enter those meetings with humility and curiosity. I listen first. I don't assume. I stay present.

Rather than defend, I look for alignment. How can we work together? What creates psychological safety here?'

Charlie's experience didn't just shape how he responded in one moment – it fundamentally shifted how he approaches leadership. It's a mindset I've seen him bring to every challenge, every conversation, and every decision we've explored together.

Leadership is filled with uncertainty, setbacks, and difficult decisions. But Stoicism provides a framework for staying grounded. It's about controlling what you can – your thoughts, emotions, and actions – and letting go of what you can't.

Challenges will come. People will misunderstand you. Plans will fail. But when you train yourself to see every obstacle as an opportunity, you become unstoppable. Not because life gets easier, but because you become stronger.

That is the power of *Amor Fati* – embracing everything, good and bad, as fuel for growth.

Reflective Questions

These questions aren't about perfect answers – they're here to help you notice where Amor Fati *might meet you in your own life and leadership.*

- Where am I resisting what is – wishing things were different, rather than working with what I have?
- What challenge or setback might hold an opportunity I haven't yet seen?
- If I believed this experience was happening for me, not to me, how would that change the way I lead?
- What would it look like to trust the path I'm on – even if I can't yet see where it leads?
- How can I meet today – exactly as it is – with acceptance, and still stay open to growth?

This is the practice: to meet life as it is, and keep growing from there.

What's Next?

In the next chapter, we explore one of the biggest barriers to *Amor Fati* – the need for control. Why we cling to it, how it limits us, and what happens when we finally let go.

Chapter 5

LEADING
BEYOND CONTROL

'In life, our first job is to divide and distinguish things into two categories: externals I cannot control, but the choices I make with regard to them I do control. Where will I find good and bad? In me, in my choices.'

– EPICTETUS[14]

Control can feel like a source of security – a way to create certainty, prevent failure, or avoid disruption. But life rarely cooperates. The more we try to hold on, the more it resists. Plans unravel. People act unpredictably. Circumstances shift overnight. And despite our best efforts, not everything is ours to manage.

When things don't go to plan, when others don't act as expected, when something derails our vision,

---

14   Paraphrased from Epictetus, *Discourses*, Book 2, Chapter 5, trans. Robert Dobbin (London: Penguin Classics, 2008).

our instinct is to tighten our grip. We try to fix it, force it back on track, or push through sheer will. But how often does this actually work? And at what cost?

For many leaders I work with, the need for control is a source of exhaustion. They are stretched too thin, trying to stay across key priorities and hold things together, making sure things run smoothly. And their desire for control doesn't come from a place of arrogance – it comes from responsibility. They care deeply about their teams, their work, and the outcomes they are accountable for.

But the irony of leadership is this: the more you try to control everything, the weaker your leadership becomes.

Control doesn't create stability – it creates stress. Leaders who hold on too tightly become reactive rather than strategic. They burn themselves out and, unintentionally, disempower those around them. The best leaders aren't the ones who monitor every detail. They are the ones who focus on what truly matters and create the space for others to step up.

So, the question isn't whether you can control everything – you can't. The real question is: How much energy are you spending trying to? And what would shift if you let go?

The Power of Discernment

This is why the Stoics placed so much emphasis on distinguishing between what is within our control and what is not. This simple but powerful distinction changes everything.

Some things are within your control: your mindset, your actions, your choices, your presence. And some things are not: other people's reactions, external events, market shifts, organisational decisions made above you. Yet, time and time again, we get caught up in frustration, anger, or anxiety over things outside our control, while giving too little attention to what *is* within our power.

This applies to life as much as it does leadership. You can't control traffic, but you can control how you show up for the meeting. You can't control whether your child listens, but you can control how you guide them. You can't control every challenge that comes your way, but you can control how you respond.

Epictetus reminds us: 'What upsets people is not things themselves, but their judgments about these things.'[15]. The way we interpret events, the meaning we assign to them, determines our experience far more than the events themselves. This is why understanding the dichotomy of control is so valuable – not just in leadership, but in life.

At the heart of this is a simple truth: your actions and your attitude are the only things fully within your control. These are shaped by your ability to discern whether a situation is something you can manage or influence. When you find yourself clinging to

---

15   Epictetus, *Enchiridion*, trans. E Carter, 1758, Section 5, public domain; adapted by the author.

control, ask yourself this critical question: Is this within my control?

If the answer is no, then what?

When something truly isn't yours to control, continuing to fight against it only leads to exhaustion, frustration, and wasted effort. The challenge is not just in recognising what is outside your control, but in accepting it. Letting go doesn't mean giving up – it means choosing to focus your time and energy where it can actually make a difference.

Sometimes, acceptance means simply stepping back. There are moments when the best action is to do nothing – to release the need to force a situation and trust that clarity will come in time. Other times, acceptance is about choosing *how* to engage rather than whether to engage at all. While you may not have control, you may still have influence. If a decision has been made above you that you disagree with, you may not be able to reverse it – but you can choose how you navigate it, how you communicate with your team, and how you adapt your approach. The ability to discern between when to step forward and when to step back is one of the most valuable leadership skills.

If the answer *is* yes – this is within my control – this is where your energy should go.

Clarity comes when you focus on your actions and attitude – on what is directly within your power.

One of my clients, Julia, a leader in a complex, high-pressure environment, learned to apply this mindset when she felt overwhelmed. She would pause and simply ask herself, 'What is my job here?' This simple question allowed her to refocus and let go of what was beyond her reach.

Julia's story is one I return to often because it captures something I believe deeply as a coach: that clarity is a form of kindness we can give ourselves[16], and others.

In coaching conversations, I often see leaders trying to manage everything around them. It's rarely about ego – more often, it comes from a deep sense of care and commitment. But that sense of responsibility can turn into over-responsibility. The shift happens when they realise they don't need to control every detail – they just need to focus their energy and attention on where it will have the most impact.

When reflecting on the question of control, remember that there will be instances where you may not have direct control, but you do have influence – and you always have control over the actions and attitude you bring to a situation. Julia's story also highlights the distinction between control and influence. Rather than giving attention to what she couldn't change, she chose to focus on what she could affect – her relationships, her clarity, and her mindset. When something didn't directly impact her work, she learned to 'park it' – choosing not to give it oxygen or attention. And when something did affect her outcomes but sat outside her control, she took a different route: she focused on the

16   B Brown, *Dare to Lead: Brave Work. Tough Conversations. Whole Hearts*, Random House, New York, 2018.

relationships that mattered. As she put it, 'If I can't control someone's behaviour but they influence my work, I pick up the phone and talk to them.'

That simple but intentional move – reaching out, having a conversation – became a practical strategy she used again and again. She remained focused on what she *could* do.

In both of these examples, Julia wasn't trying to control everything. She was clear about what belonged to her – and just as importantly, what didn't. That clarity freed up energy and gave her permission to let go of the rest.

She didn't feel trapped by situations she couldn't change. She didn't exhaust herself over what was outside her grasp. Instead, she freed herself to focus on what truly made a difference.

The Fear That Fuels Control

Letting go of control can stir up discomfort. It touches something very human – the desire for certainty, for safety, for a sense of order in the chaos. Even when we understand the value of letting go, actually doing it can feel vulnerable. But it's in those moments that we begin to build trust – in ourselves, and in those around us. It often stirs up feelings of uncertainty and vulnerability, which makes it hard to step back – even when we know we should. Underneath it all, the drive to control is usually fuelled by a desire for security: to know what's coming, to avoid mistakes, to hold onto some sense of stability in an unpredictable world. But the truth is, much of life – and leadership – is inherently uncertain.

In coaching conversations, this theme comes up often. Leaders talk about the pressure to have the answers, to keep everything on track, to protect their team from mistakes. It usually comes from a good place – a sense of care, commitment, and responsibility. But over time, that pressure starts to wear them down. They feel stretched thin, constantly responsible for everyone and everything. And often, without meaning to, they create teams that wait for direction rather than stepping up with initiative.

This is how control often shows up. Sometimes it looks like micromanagement or over-planning. Other times, it's hesitation – the urge to wait until everything feels just right before making a move. Whether it's jumping in too fast or holding back too long, the root is often the same: a fear of not knowing, not being ready, not having certainty.

Take a moment to consider: Where does your need for control show up? Do you struggle to delegate, worried things won't be done 'right'? Do you find yourself holding off on decisions until you feel totally prepared? Becoming aware of these patterns is the first step to loosening their grip.

The shift usually begins with curiosity. Leaders start saying things like, 'I don't have the answer – what do you think?' It sounds simple, but it's a powerful move. Teams respond. Engagement lifts. People start stepping into more ownership. And leaders begin to reclaim energy and space – to focus on what really matters.

What if, instead of fearing uncertainty, we made room for it? What if we stopped trying to control everything, and started focusing on how we show up in the face of the unknown? We may not always control the situation, but we always have a say in our response.

The Freedom in Letting Go

When we let go of the need to control, we don't become passive – we learn to accept what is. We begin to see where our energy is best spent, where we have real influence, and where we need to step back.

Marcus Aurelius reminds us: 'You have power over your mind – not outside events. Realise this, and you will find strength.'[17] His words invite us to pause and consider: Where are we placing our energy? How much of our stress, frustration, or exhaustion comes not from what's happening around us, but from our resistance to it?

I was reminded of this when I lost my hearing overnight (the story I shared in the opening of this book). In the uncertainty of those first days, I wrestled with questions, searching for explanations, hoping for a return to normal. But once I had the answer – that my hearing wasn't coming back – I faced a choice. I could stay caught in frustration over something I couldn't change, or I could shift my focus to what was within my control.

17   M Aurelius, *Meditations*, trans. G Long, 1862, public domain.

That shift changed everything. I researched cochlear implants. I explored what support was available. I became intentional about my mindset and the way I showed up for myself and others. Most importantly, I asked myself: How do I want to experience myself in this situation? How do I want others to experience me? Those questions anchored me in action – not in what I had lost, but in what I could do moving forward. And it was in those small, deliberate steps that I started to feel like myself again.

Shifting our focus from external to internal control is not about abandoning direction or action. We still set goals, clarify priorities, and make plans – but we do so with the understanding that while we can influence outcomes, we cannot guarantee them. What we *can* control is the next step we take, the choices we make, and the way we accept, and then respond to, what unfolds.

This isn't a lesson learned once. It's an ongoing practice – one that requires awareness, discipline, and the ability to pause before reacting. Craving control doesn't disappear overnight, but each time you catch yourself grasping at what isn't yours to hold, you create an opportunity – to reflect, reset, and ask yourself: What really matters here?

And that is all we ever truly control – our actions and our attitude.

That's the paradox: the less you try to control everything, the more power you actually have.

Closing Reflection:
WHAT ARE YOU HOLDING ON TO?

Letting go of control doesn't mean stepping away from leadership – it means stepping into it more fully. But before that, it often starts on a more personal level. Beneath the responsibilities and expectations is a human being navigating uncertainty, doing their best to manage what's theirs and let go of what's not. That inner work matters just as much as the outer leadership.

As a leader, your role isn't to control every outcome. It's to provide a clear direction – a north star – and then invite others to find their own way of contributing. When you lead with that kind of intention, you offer your team both purpose and permission: purpose in knowing what matters, and permission to bring their own initiative to how the work gets done.

The real shift happens when you trust yourself enough to release what doesn't belong to you – and trust others enough to carry what does. That's where sustainable leadership begins: not in holding everything, but in knowing what to hold, what to share, and what to let go.

LETTING GO TO LEAD WELL

When I interviewed Rani – a senior public servant I coached a few years ago and have stayed in contact with – I was reminded of one of the most important leadership shifts we can make: letting go of control, without letting go of clarity or responsibility.

As an Assistant Commissioner in the Strategic Programs Office, Rani works in a large, complex public sector environment where the stakes are high and visibility is constant. But what makes her insights so powerful is that they're rooted not just in her role, but in her personal story.

> *'At 24, I lost my mother. It changed everything. Her passing made me acutely aware that life doesn't wait, and that time – whether in our personal or professional lives – is never guaranteed. I realised then: I don't want to waste time on things that don't matter.'*

That perspective has shaped the way she leads. Rani talks about her ongoing practice of returning to what matters most – especially when complexity or pressure starts to cloud her judgment.

> *'Whatever challenge I'm facing, I remind myself: this is not the worst thing that could happen. It helps me recalibrate. It helps me focus on what is actually within my control.'*

Still, she's the first to admit that it's not always easy.

> *'That doesn't mean I don't get caught up in the noise. I do. I get tripped up on control, especially*

when the pressure is high – when the stakes are big, the consequences are real, and too many people are watching. That's when it's easy to let stress dictate my actions, to get caught in the illusion that if I just push harder, I can control the outcome.

I know that pattern in myself. I've had to train myself to pause and ask:

"What is my job here? What can I actually influence? And what do I need to let go of?"

I can't control how others will react, but I can control how I lead.'

And when she feels herself slipping – over-focusing on something, losing the bigger picture, or getting stuck in her own head – she turns to the people around her.

'I'm lucky – I have a trusted peer group. They bring me back in when I need it. If I'm fixated on a problem, I'll walk down the hallway and chat with someone I trust. I remember sitting at my desk late one afternoon, stressing about something, and I called my line manager. She didn't even get into the issue with me. She just asked about my upcoming holiday and other unrelated stuff. And it worked – when I hung up, I'd stopped spiralling and I went home!'

That moment stuck with her because it revealed something important.

'That's the thing about control – it tricks you into believing you're the only one who can fix everything. But leadership isn't about carrying the weight alone.

The best thing I've done is let people really get to know me – so they can tell when I'm slipping into control mode and call it out.'

For Rani, control isn't just about managing tasks – it's about managing focus.

'I've learned that control is about discipline, not force. If I don't manage my focus, I risk spending too much time on one issue and neglecting other parts of my portfolio. I start thinking about work outside the office, I stop sleeping, and my routine breaks down. I lose perspective.'

She shared one piece of advice that has stuck with her since stepping into her current role:

'Anchor your energy on what is good for your business.

It's so easy to get caught up in things that feel urgent but don't really matter. That's why I'm deliberate about where I spend my time. I make sure my team understands the bigger picture. I encourage them to build relationships beyond their immediate area. When people widen their view, they broaden their perspective, and make better decisions.'

She also knows how important it is to help people feel connected to what they do – even when the work isn't always visible.

'I can't always talk about my work outside of it. My dad's 76 – he thinks I just chat on the phone all day. He doesn't see the weight of what I carry. That's true

for a lot of people in my team, too. Their work is often behind the scenes. It's easy to forget how much it matters. So, it's my job to remind them.'

It's one of the many places her leadership shines: helping others reconnect with meaning and pride in their contribution.

'The way people perceive their role shapes how they show up. If they see it as just a list of tasks, they disengage. But if they understand the impact of what they do, the way it shapes the system, they take pride in it. And that pride? That's what keeps good people in roles that matter.'

Letting go of control hasn't made Rani less effective. It's made her more present, more connected, and more intentional. And that's the paradox we've explored in this chapter: when you stop trying to hold everything, you gain something far more powerful – clarity, trust, and the freedom to lead from a place of purpose.

Reflective Questions

These questions offer a framework to help you navigate what's within your control – and what isn't. They aren't a checklist to complete. They're here to help you focus your attention where it matters most.

As you reflect, consider:

Where might control be holding me back? Where might letting go help me see things more clearly, stay focused, or take more useful action?

Define What's Truly in Your Control

- What part of this situation depends entirely on my actions, choices, or mindset?
- Can I directly influence or change the outcome, or am I hoping for others or external events to align?

Separate Internal from External

- Is this an external event (other people's decisions or circumstances), or internal (my response, interpretation, or effort)?
- If I step back, am I trying to control something inherently outside my power – like someone else's opinion or reaction?

Focus on What You Can Do

- What proactive steps can I take right now, within my control?

- Am I spending more energy worrying about results than refining my intention and process?

Detach from the Outcome

- If I let go of the need to control this, how would that change how I feel or act?
- What's the worst-case scenario – and could I still manage my response to it?

Letting go of control isn't about stepping back – it's about stepping forward with greater clarity.

Each time you pause and reflect, you strengthen your ability to focus on what matters.

What's Next?

The next chapter turns to a critical Stoic idea: Perception – the lens through which we interpret and respond to what life throws our way. Because once we understand that our perception shapes our reality, we realise that real power doesn't come from controlling the world – it comes from the way we choose to see it.

Chapter 6

PERCEPTION – REWRITING THE STORIES WE TELL OURSELVES

'It is not events that upset us but rather our opinions about them.'

– EPICTETUS[18]

We rarely see the world as it is – we see it as we are. Our experiences, emotions, and biases shape the way we interpret events. What one person sees as an exciting challenge, another may view as an impossible hurdle. The same situation can trigger frustration in one person and curiosity in another. The difference is not in the event itself, but in the perception of it.

This distinction matters. Perception impacts everything. It dictates how we respond to difficulties,

---

18   Epictetus, *Enchiridion*, trans. E Carter, 1758, Section 5, public domain; adapted by the author.

how we interpret setbacks, and how we navigate our lives. When we shift our perception, we shift our experience – and that shift is always within our control.

But taking control of perception requires awareness. It means recognising that our thoughts are not facts but interpretations. It means questioning whether the stories we tell ourselves serve us or hold us back. And it means stepping back from the immediate emotion of a moment to see the bigger picture.

The Lens Through Which We See

The Stoics understood that our suffering often comes not from external events, but from our judgments about them.

> 'You have power over your mind – not outside events. Realise this, and you will find strength.' – Marcus Aurelius[19]

This is a liberating truth: while we cannot always control what happens to us, we can control how we interpret and respond to it.

But our brains are not wired for this kind of calm clarity. They're wired for survival. Designed to detect threats and react quickly, our minds can easily misread modern situations as dangers. A delayed reply. A sharp email. A sudden change. These things are rarely life-threatening, but they often trigger strong reactions.

Perception is like wearing sunglasses. The lens we look through is coloured by our past experiences, our

---

19   M Aurelius, *Meditations* (Long, 1862), Book 6, Section 8.

current emotions, and the stories we tell ourselves. Just as you can take off sunglasses to see more clearly, you can learn to take a step back and question your thinking.

That's exactly what happened for Moira, a senior leader I worked with who had just been reassigned to a new team. The move wasn't her choice – and at first, it felt like a loss. She'd built deep trust and a strong sense of momentum in her previous role, and this transition felt like a sudden interruption.

Her internal dialogue was clear: I don't belong here. This isn't fair. This wasn't my choice. The story she was telling herself shaped her entire experience – it drained her energy and coloured how she showed up with the new team.

In our coaching sessions, we explored what she could and couldn't control. As we slowed things down, she began to notice the narrative running in the background. With a bit of distance, she asked herself different questions: What might this team need from me? What can I bring? How can I make this work for me, not just something happening to me? She became more deliberate about the story she told – both to herself and to others.

The external event didn't change. But her perception did – and that changed everything. Her energy lifted. Her engagement grew. She shifted from feeling disoriented to feeling grounded. She brought clarity, direction, and fresh momentum – not just to the work, but to the team around her.

That's the power of perception.

The Stories We Tell Ourselves

We all carry stories about who we are and how the world works. Some serve us. Others keep us stuck. These narratives don't just shape our professional decisions – they shape our self-image, our confidence, and our sense of agency.

A person who believes, *I always struggle with change*, will approach transitions with hesitation. A person who believes, *I find ways to adapt*, will approach uncertainty with more openness.

Carl Jung is often quoted as saying, 'Until you make the unconscious conscious, it will direct your life and you will call it fate.'[20] When we bring our internal narratives into the light, we can decide whether to keep them or rewrite them.

From Reaction to Reflection

Mastering perception isn't about pretending everything is fine or suppressing emotion. It's about choosing how you respond. Emotions are signals, not instructions. They tell you what matters, but they don't have to control what you do.

That's where the pause comes in. As Viktor Frankl, a Holocaust survivor and psychiatrist, taught: Between stimulus and response lies a space. In that space is our

---

20　This quote is widely attributed to Carl Jung, though no definitive source in his published works has been identified. It is often cited as reflecting key Jungian ideas on the unconscious and personal development.

power to choose our response. In our response lies our growth and our freedom.[21]

This space holds our ability to reframe, to choose, and to shift the story we tell ourselves.

When something goes wrong, ask yourself: Is my perception helping me or hindering me? Is there another way to see this?

Perceptive Leaders Lead Differently

How we interpret situations doesn't just shape our experience – it shapes how we lead.

Leaders who pause, reflect, and reframe are better equipped to navigate complexity. They don't jump to conclusions. They don't assume the worst. They don't confuse a temporary setback for a permanent failure.

They notice their assumptions and challenge them. They choose curiosity over certainty. And they understand that what they see is always a filtered version of reality.

One leader I worked with shared this simple shift: 'When a team member goes quiet in a meeting, I no longer assume they're disengaged. I ask myself: could something else be going on?' That small pause changes the tone of the follow-up conversation – and often uncovers something important.

The way you see influences the way you lead.

---

21   This passage is widely attributed to Viktor E Frankl and reflects key ideas from *Man's Search for Meaning*, Beacon Press, Boston, 2006. It does not appear verbatim in his published works.

Closing Reflection:
CHOOSING A NEW FRAME

Perception isn't about seeing the world through rose-coloured glasses. It's about seeing clearly – without distortion, without assumption, without being a prisoner to old narratives. It's about choosing a frame that serves you rather than limits you.

A challenge can be a burden or an opportunity. A failure can be an endpoint or a lesson. A setback can be a sign to quit or a nudge to grow. The event remains the same. The meaning is yours to define.

This ability to step back, reframe, and choose a perception that serves you is one of the most powerful skills for both life and leadership. It allows you to move forward with clarity rather than being stuck in frustration. It enables you to lead with intention rather than reaction.

And it prepares you for what comes next.

SEEING CLEARLY IN UNCERTAINTY

When I sat down to interview Mira for this book – a Director working in a national public sector strategy team – I was reminded how deeply perception shapes our experience of leadership. Mira had recently transitioned from one agency to another, stepping into a leadership role in a team facing ongoing restructures, shifting priorities, and persistent uncertainty.

Her story is one of calm leadership – not because the circumstances were calm, but because she learned how to reframe her experience, choose her response, and support her team with steadiness.

> *'Leading in an organisation going through constant change can feel like being in the middle of an ocean with no land in sight. The waves keep coming… and my challenge was to be the steady force for my team, even when I had no control over what was coming next.'*

Like many leaders, Mira once believed strength meant showing no doubt. But through experience – and through coaching – she began to see that *perception* was the key to navigating the storm.

> *'Real strength isn't about pretending to have control. It's about knowing what is within my control, letting go of the rest, and helping my team do the same. And most importantly, it's about managing how I see the situation – because my perception shapes my ability to lead through it.'*

One of the biggest shifts for Mira came when she stopped resisting change and started responding to it.

> *'I used to think being a leader meant projecting confidence at all times. But I've realised that acknowledging reality – rather than resisting it – makes me a stronger leader.'*

Instead of pushing through or covering up the tension her team was feeling, she chose transparency.

> *'When my team was struggling, instead of pretending everything was fine, I started to say: "Yes, this is tough. Yes, I feel it too. But here's what we can do right now."'*

This reframing – grounded in honesty and presence – helped shift how her team experienced uncertainty. Her perception became their anchor.

Mira described what many leaders experience: being the person others bring their stress to, while still trying to hold everything steady.

> *'Leadership means being in the middle of the storm,while others come to you with their fear and frustration.'*

What changed for her wasn't the pressure – but how she chose to see it. Instead of internalising every emotion or trying to fix everything, she learned to stay grounded.

> *'I used to think that showing any emotion would make me look weak. Now, I see that acknowledging challenges – without spiralling into negativity – is what helps people trust you.'*

Mira shared the metaphor she often uses: 'seeing from the balcony'. The practice of stepping back – not to detach, but to see more clearly.

> *'It's easy to get caught up in the day-to-day chaos. But when I step back, I can ask: "What can I actually control in this situation? Where should*

I focus my energy? What blockers can I work around?'"

That shift in perception changes everything. Instead of reacting from frustration, she responds with clarity.

In this chapter, we've explored how perception shapes the way we interpret others. Mira put this into practice by choosing where to place her energy.

'I've learned that not every battle is worth fighting, and not every perception can be change. Instead of wasting energy trying to change people's minds, I focus on what's possible – like creating a healthy team environment.'

It's a grounded, emotionally intelligent approach that acknowledges reality without getting stuck in it.

During our conversation, Mira reflected on how she stayed steady across long periods of uncertainty. Her answer was simple but powerful: she stopped trying to fix everything and started focusing on small wins.

'Working closely with someone I hadn't known before and building a strong working relationship – that was a win. Supporting a colleague through a tough time – that was a win.'

These wins weren't always measurable – but they shaped the emotional tone of her team.

Mira also described one of her biggest turning points: realising that trying to carry everything alone wasn't sustainable.

'There were times when I felt like I was running on empty... That's when I learned leadership doesn't mean doing it alone.'

Coaching helped her see a pattern she hadn't fully recognised before.

'I mapped out how I was spending my time and realised I was pouring everything into work and leaving no time to recharge. That awareness changed everything.'

By shifting her focus, she began leading with more clarity and less fatigue.

As we wrapped up our conversation, Mira said something that perfectly captured the essence of this chapter:

'In the end, it all comes back to perception. How I see a situation shapes how I handle it – and how my team experiences it. When I step back, focus on what I can control, and let go of the rest, I can lead with more steadiness and less stress.'

Her story reminds us: perception isn't just a mindset – it's a leadership practice. And when we shift the story we tell ourselves, we change the way we show up for others.

Reflective Questions

As a leader, the questions you ask yourself shape the way you lead. These prompts are here to support your perspective – especially in challenging moments, when you need to guide your team, stay steady, or gain clarity.

See the Bigger Picture

- What will this decision or situation mean for my team, organisation, or stakeholders a year from now? Five years from now?
- If I were observing this from a strategic, whole-of-system perspective, what patterns, opportunities, or risks might I notice?
- Am I focusing my energy on what truly drives results, or getting caught in operational minutiae?

See Your Growth

- What leadership lesson can I take from this experience, regardless of the outcome?
- How have I handled similar challenges in the past, and what insight can I carry forward?
- Am I leading in alignment with my values, vision, and long-term goals?

See Through Other Eyes

- How might my team, peers, or stakeholders view this differently?
- Am I giving others the benefit of the doubt and assuming positive intent?
- If a trusted advisor, coach, or mentor were in my shoes, what might they suggest?

See with Emotional Clarity

- What emotions am I experiencing most strongly, and how might they be influencing me?
- How would I respond if I were less emotionally invested – or more objective?
- Am I reacting instinctively, or responding with thoughtfulness and intention?

See What's Good

- What am I grateful for in this situation, even amidst the challenges?
- What potential opportunities or growth could emerge from this?
- How can I use this experience to strengthen my leadership?

These questions aren't about having all the answers – they're here to help you pause, widen your lens, and lead with greater clarity, steadiness, and intent.

What's Next?

Perception is power – but it's only the first step. Seeing clearly is essential, but what comes next matters just as much.

How you respond to what you see – how you regulate, decide, and take action – determines everything. That's where we turn next: the discipline of self-regulation. Because if perception shapes your experience, self-discipline shapes your choices.

Chapter 7

THE ROLE OF REASON – LEADING YOURSELF FIRST

'No man is free who is not a master of himself.'

– EPICTETUS[22]

If perception shapes our experience, self-discipline shapes our choices. The ability to pause before reacting, steady emotions, and choose a response is the foundation of an anchored mindset.

Yet, in moments of stress, frustration, or uncertainty, self-control can feel out of reach. A sharp email lands in your inbox. A last-minute decision disrupts months of planning. A colleague takes credit for your work. In these moments, emotion rises fast, and the pull to react is strong. But when we act on impulse, we often create more harm – to relationships, to our credibility, and to our own sense of steadiness.

22   Epictetus, *Discourses*, trans. T W Higginson, 1865, Book 2, Chapter 10, public domain.

The Stoics understood this well. They didn't expect people to shut off their emotions – but they did believe we always have a choice in how we respond. Emotional control isn't about pushing feelings aside or pretending they don't exist. It's about recognising emotions for what they are – indicators, not instructions – and deciding what to do with them.

This is the difference between reacting and leading.

The Two Phases of Emotion

The Stoic philosopher Epictetus described two phases of emotional response.[23]

The first phase is the immediate reaction. It is automatic and instinctive – a surge of frustration, a moment of fear, a tightening in the chest. This phase is natural and unavoidable. Even the most disciplined person will feel emotions arise.

The second phase is the conscious evaluation. This is where choice enters the picture. Do we let the initial emotion dictate our response? Or do we pause, assess, and choose a more measured approach?

Many of us confuse these two phases, believing that because we feel something, we must act on it. But there is always a choice between emotion and response. The key is to recognise this gap and train ourselves to step into it.

---

23 Epictetus, *Discourses*, Book 4, Chapter 1. This passage is paraphrased from ideas expressed in modern translations, including R Dobbin, *Discourses*, Penguin Classics, London, 2008.

This concept aligns closely with *The Chimp Paradox*, a model developed by Professor Steve Peters, a consultant psychiatrist who has worked with elite athletes and business leaders to improve performance and emotional management[24]. It suggests that we have two key forces within us:

- The Chimp, which represents our emotional, instinctive brain – reactive, impulsive, and driven by fear or frustration.
- The Human, which is our rational, logical brain – calm, thoughtful, and goal-oriented.

When we react immediately, it's often our Chimp that is in control. The key to self-discipline is learning to manage the Chimp – acknowledging its presence but allowing our Human brain to take charge.

Separating Emotion from Response

The ability to pause, steady yourself, and choose your response – this is a common focus area in my coaching work.

Many leaders are capable, experienced, and thoughtful – until stress takes over. When something goes wrong, it's easy to react instantly. A sharp email sent too quickly. A conversation shut down. A decision made from frustration rather than clarity.

---

24   S Peters, *The Chimp Paradox: The Mind Management Programme to Help You Achieve Success, Confidence and Happiness*, Vermilion, London, 2012.

In the moment, it feels like control – but over time, these reactions can erode trust and connection within a team.

The shift often begins with something simple: a pause.

Before responding, I encourage leaders to take a breath and ask themselves: 'What outcome do I actually want here?'

It sounds small – but this pause changes everything. It creates space to engage with curiosity rather than defensiveness. It creates room to seek clarity before reacting. It helps leaders choose responses that align with their values, rather than their frustration.

This is what emotional discipline looks like in practice.

It's also what *The Chimp Paradox* model describes so well. In those reactive moments, it's often the Chimp – the emotional, instinctive brain – that's in charge. The work is not to silence the Chimp, but to create space for the Human – the rational, thoughtful mind – to step in and lead.

I've experienced this myself – on the padel court.

When I first started, I'd find myself spiralling if I wasn't playing well. If I missed a few shots or made mistakes, my inner critic would flare up fast. Thoughts like 'Why am I even playing this game? I'm no good at it. My partner must be frustrated to be playing with me.' Those thoughts would take over before I even realised what was happening.

And of course, the more I spiralled, the worse I played.

I had to teach myself to interrupt that pattern. To dust myself off. To take one point at a time.

These days, I use intentional self-talk – words like 'steady and strong' or 'next point' – to bring myself back into the moment. To stay grounded. To respond rather than react.

It's exactly the same practice I see in leadership – learning to manage the voice in your head so you can stay steady in the moment in front of you.

And like anything worth practising, it doesn't stop with one moment, or one situation.

Learning to separate emotion from response is ongoing work – in sport, in leadership, in life. There will always be days where frustration shows up. Where things don't go to plan.

But this is where Stoic practice offers us something powerful – a reminder that obstacles aren't just disruptions to overcome. They're part of the path. They're what shape us.

Embracing Obstacles Strengthens Emotional Discipline

As we explored in chapter three, the core Stoic principle, *Amor Fati* – the love of fate – reminds us to embrace obstacles as part of the journey rather than as disruptions. If we see difficulties as something to resist, they will provoke frustration, anxiety, or even despair. But if we choose to accept challenges as part of the process, our emotional response changes.

This shift in perspective has a direct impact on self-discipline. When setbacks happen – when a project fails, a decision backfires, or circumstances change unexpectedly – we can see them as opportunities to strengthen our inner resolve. This doesn't mean pretending hardship is easy, but it does mean refusing to let it dictate our emotions. A disciplined mind learns to meet obstacles with acceptance rather than resistance.

The Mind-Body Connection

Our emotions don't just exist in the mind; they show up in the body. Stress tightens the shoulders. Anxiety creates restlessness. Frustration speeds up the heart rate.

The Stoics recognised this link between body and mind. They believed that physical discipline supported mental discipline. Seneca advised, 'We treat the body rigorously so that it will not be disobedient to the mind.'[25]

In my own life, since embracing Stoicism, I see small acts of physical discipline – regular strength and cardio training – as a way to strengthen my ability to override short-term discomfort for long-term benefit. To endure physical discomfort so I can build the mental muscle to withstand emotional and psychological challenges when they arise. I also see this as a way to set myself up with wins every day. If I say I'm going to the gym, and I go, I've set myself up with a win for the day.

25 Seneca, *Moral Letters to Lucilius*, Letter 15, trans. R.M. Gummere, Loeb Classical Library, Harvard University Press, Cambridge, 1917.

I have friends who run ultra marathons and have completed Iron Man events. That isn't me. But small wins every day – doing something hard – strengthen my resolve and my self-belief that I can handle difficult things.

For leaders, this means acknowledging the connection between body and mind. It means recognising that when you prioritise your well-being, you are setting yourself up to think clearly, make better decisions, and lead more effectively. It means understanding that self-discipline in any form – whether it's waking up early, maintaining a workout routine, or simply choosing to take a walk when frustration builds – strengthens your capacity for emotional control.

When emotions run high, the body offers a way to reset. Taking a walk, stepping outside, or even just standing up and stretching can interrupt an emotional spiral and restore a sense of steadiness. The path to mental strength is built, in part, through the discipline of the body.

The Power of Small Wins

James Clear, in *Atomic Habits*[26], argues that every action we take is a vote for the person we want to become. Self-discipline is not about willpower; it is about momentum.

---

26   Clear, *Atomic Habits*, 2018.

Teresa Amabile and Steven Kramer, researchers in organisational psychology, found in their work on *The Progress Principle*[27] that small, meaningful progress fuels emotional well-being. Even minor steps forward boost engagement and confidence, while setbacks – no matter how small – can have an outsized negative effect.

Roger Federer, one of the greatest tennis players in history, provides an example of this in action. In a commencement speech[28], he shared that while he won 80% of the matches he played, he only won 54% of the points. He didn't dwell on lost points or carry frustration into the next one. He simply reset and refocused; playing the next point with full intention.

The best leaders do the same. They don't get stuck in past mistakes or emotional reactions. They course-correct, focus on the next decision, and move forward.

The key to self-control is not waiting for motivation but focusing on small, consistent actions that align with who you want to become. If you feel stuck, overwhelmed, or reactive, the best thing you can do is take one deliberate step forward – a step that reinforces the identity you are building.

---

27   Teresa Amabile and Steven Kramer, *The Progress Principle: Using Small Wins to Ignite Joy, Engagement, and Creativity at Work* (Boston: Harvard Business Review Press, 2011).
28   R Federer, 'Commencement Address at Dartmouth College', *Dartmouth College*, 9 June 2024, accessed 17 April 2025, https://home.dartmouth.edu/news/2024/06/commencement-address-roger-federer.

Closing Reflection:
THE PATH FORWARD

Self-discipline is not about suppression or rigidity. It's about clarity – knowing what is within your control and developing the ability to respond with intention rather than impulse. It's about recognising emotions as signals, not instructions. It's about building the habit of pausing, steadying yourself, and moving forward in a way that aligns with the leader you want to be.

Some days, this might mean taking a breath before responding. Other days, it might mean stepping away from a situation to regain perspective. It could be as simple as shifting your focus to the next small action, the next conversation, the next point played. Over time, these small choices compound, reinforcing the identity of someone who leads with reason rather than reactivity.

One of the most effective ways to steady yourself in uncertain times is to shift your focus from what is lacking to what is present. Just as self-discipline shapes the way we respond, gratitude strengthens and shapes the way we see.

HOLDING STEADY UNDER PRESSURE

When I interviewed Tara for this book – a seasoned Executive Director – I was struck by how naturally her leadership philosophy embodied the Stoic principle we explored in Chapter 7: You can't control the world, but you can have self-control.

Tara has held senior roles for many years, but she's quick to point out that leadership authority doesn't shield you from pressure. In fact, the stakes only get higher.

> *'As I've taken on senior leadership roles, I've gained more influence and decision-making power – but with that comes immense pressure and responsibility. Holding these two things together – formal authority and intense stress – can be a slippery slope if you're not careful.'*

One of the tensions we explored in this chapter is the paradox of responsibility: when you hold power, you must also hold yourself steady. Without emotional regulation, leadership can easily tip into reaction or control. As Tara reflected, staying grounded is not just a helpful trait – it's essential.

> *'Staying grounded is what keeps me steady, and over the years, I've developed a few ways to do that.'*

Tara's awareness of ego, and how easily it can sneak into decision-making, aligns with one of the central ideas of

Stoic self-discipline: being intentional in how you use your influence.

> *'I constantly ask myself whether my decisions are coming from real reflection or if I'm leaning too much on my role and status. Am I focusing on what's right, or just trying to be right?'*

That question – am I trying to be right, or do what's right – is one of the most powerful tools for keeping ego in check. Tara keeps perspective by staying connected to people outside of her professional world – people who see her not as a leader, but as a person.

> *'I rely on the people in my life who keep me real – family, old friends, and a broader community who don't care about my title. They remind me that I am more than my job. My adult kids, especially, keep me humble when they tell me to stop working so we can share a meal together and chat. It's a good reality check!'*

What she's describing here is an intentional shift in identity – something we talked about in the chapter through the lens of James Clear's habit formation: every action is a vote for who you're becoming. For Tara, that means not just being a leader, but a grounded human first.

> *'One of the biggest lessons I've learned is that control is an illusion. You can lose anything – your job, your health, your sense of stability – in an instant.'*

This mindset allows her to lead with humility and perspective. It also strengthens her ability to respond, rather than react.

Tara shared a moment, one that offered a powerful leadership lesson. During a team workshop, she misread how people would show up.

> 'I had assumed the team would join the workshop online, but when I logged in, I found that almost everyone was in the office in our usual meeting room. I was one of the few sitting at my screen, along with our remote guest presenter and a few remote staff. Facilitating discussion from a screen while most of the group was in the room felt awkward and isolating.'

Instead of getting frustrated or defensive, she reflected on what the moment had to teach her. That's what Stoic self-discipline looks like in action.

> 'This experience gave me some insight into the unintended participation barriers of hybrid meetings. So, at our next meeting, I sat closest to the screen. I directed my attention to the remote participants first and asked them deliberate questions to get their input. I finished the session by sharing why I had taken this approach; it was a valuable lesson for us all.'

What I love about this story is that it shows how emotional control isn't always about high-stakes conflict – it can also look like humility, presence, and a willingness to adapt.

Tara also spoke about the physical and emotional toll of leadership. As we discussed in Chapter 7, stress lives in the body – and discipline isn't just mental. It's physical, too.

> *'Leadership puts you in high-pressure situations where emotions run high – whether it's a tough conversation, an angry staff member, or an intense negotiation. The more someone escalates, the more I try to intentionally lower my energy and respond with calm.'*

That phrase – lowering your energy – captures a practice the Stoics would've recognised: steadying your own emotions as a way of regulating the temperature in the room.

> *'I've been in situations where I've had to dig deep – like responding to hours of technical questioning during an external review. The stress was immense, but I knew that my best tool was self-regulation. Slowing down, breathing, and maintaining composure made all the difference.'*

Tara also recognises that emotional discipline isn't only personal – it's cultural. Leaders set the tone, and team environments must support emotional steadiness if they're going to perform under pressure.

> *'If we want truly diverse, high-performing teams, we need to create environments that support emotional regulation. That means fostering trust, understanding individual needs, and creating cultures where people feel psychologically safe.'*

Part of Tara's approach to sustaining perspective is deliberately stepping outside of work to reconnect with herself. We explored this in the chapter through the idea of small wins and intentional habits. For Tara, this looks like creative rituals that anchor her outside her role.

> 'One of the best decisions I made was building routines that have nothing to do with work. For me, that includes visiting art galleries. Walking through a gallery in silence, absorbing creativity, and stepping into a different world – it's both soothing and inspiring. It reminds me that I am not just 'my role', but a person with broader interests and a need for balance.'

She's even brought this to her team – not in a theoretical way, but as a practice.

> 'Some of my staff now go to the gallery as part of team development days. It's an opportunity to step outside their usual environment, and connect with diverse cultures and each other in a different way.'

As our conversation drew to a close, Tara returned to one of the themes that sits at the heart of Stoic leadership:

> 'At the core of my leadership philosophy is a simple truth: stay anchored. Power and stress can be a dangerous mix, but if I can keep my ego in check, maintain perspective, regulate my emotions, and stay connected to life outside of work, I lead with more clarity and integrity.'

And then she added a final insight – one that resonates strongly with me:

> *'I remind myself every day – none of this is permanent. True leadership isn't about control or authority – it's about staying steady, making deliberate choices, and remembering that in the end, who you are matters more than any title you hold.'*

That, to me, is what anchored leadership looks like in practice. Not perfect, not polished – steady, deliberate, and deeply human.

Reflective Questions

Self-discipline and emotional control aren't about perfection – they're daily practices of awareness, steadiness, and choice. These questions help you pause and lead with greater clarity, especially under pressure.

Pause and Notice

- What situations trigger my strongest emotional reactions?
- When do I find myself most likely to react rather than respond?
- What physical or emotional signals tell me I need to pause?

Choose Your Response

- What outcome do I actually want here – beyond my immediate reaction?
- Am I acting from curiosity and care, or from frustration and control?
- What would a more grounded response look like in this situation?

Strengthen Daily Practices

- What small habits help me stay anchored and steady outside of work?
- Where am I building small wins that reinforce who I want to become?

- How can I support emotional steadiness within my team – not just in myself?

Staying anchored isn't about shutting down emotion – it's about learning to meet it with awareness, intention, and choice.

What's Next?

In the next chapter, we'll explore how gratitude isn't just about appreciation – it's a powerful tool in leadership and life. It sharpens focus, cuts through negativity, and keeps you anchored when pressure builds. It helps you stay engaged in the work that matters, instead of getting stuck in frustration or fixating on what's outside your control.

Chapter 8

GRATITUDE – THE STOIC'S GATEWAY TO STRENGTH AND PERSPECTIVE

'Gratitude is not only the greatest of virtues,
but the parent of all the others.'

– CICERO[29]

Gratitude is often misunderstood. It's easy to see it as something warm – a virtue for good times, a reflection when life is going well and success is evident. But the Stoics saw it differently.

They knew that gratitude is not about feeling good when everything is easy. It's about how you face life when things *aren't* going your way. It's about how you respond when plans fall apart, when setbacks hit, when pressure is relentless. Gratitude isn't just a pleasant idea – it's a tool. It sharpens perspective, stops you from

---

29   M T Cicero, *Pro Plancio*, 54 BCE, Section 82, public domain.

getting stuck in negativity, and keeps you from being consumed by what you *don't* have. It's what steadies you in the reality you're in, rather than the one you wish you had.

If gratitude only shows up when life is easy, it's more of a reflection than a practice. True gratitude is what steadies us when things are hard.

Gratitude as a Discipline, Not a Feeling

The Stoics never saw gratitude as something passive. It wasn't about waiting for life to go well –it was about choosing how to see what's already present. As Epictetus wrote, 'He is a wise man who does not grieve for the things which he has not, but rejoices for those which he has.'[30] Gratitude, for the Stoics, was an active discipline. A way of seeing clearly, not sentimentally.

This is an important distinction. Gratitude isn't just about feeling thankful when good things happen. It's about choosing to see what is already there. It's about anchoring in reality rather than focusing on what's missing.

One of my executive clients put it this way: 'To be honest, my work is my gratitude practice. I'm thankful every single day for the difference we make in our clients' lives. And for working alongside my extraordinary staff, who do this hard work with such grace and compassion. I don't want it to sound lofty,

---

30 Commonly attributed to Epictetus; reflects themes from *Discourses* and the *Enchiridion*, though not a direct quote.

Sheila, but the work itself pulls me back to earth and gives me a wake-up call whenever I drift.'

This is gratitude in action – not something reserved for a quiet moment of reflection, but something embedded in the work itself. Gratitude doesn't detach us from challenges; it grounds us in their meaning. It is not a separate exercise, but a way of moving through life. Not reserved for the end of the day, but woven into our days – and the work itself.

The Harder Gratitude

Gratitude is easy when things are going well. The real test is whether you can hold onto it when things are *not*.

This is where it intersects with *Amor Fati* – the Stoic practice of embracing life *as it is*, not just as we want it to be. Marcus Aurelius wrote: 'Convince yourself that everything is the gift of the gods, that things are good and always will be.'[31]

The idea isn't to pretend that struggle isn't difficult. It's to see that even hardship is shaping you into something stronger.

- The difficult colleague? Thank you for teaching me how to communicate better.
- The missed opportunity? Thank it for encouraging you to refine your focus.
- The headache? Thank you for making me slow down and take a break.

31   M Aurelius, *Meditations*, adapted from the public domain translation by G Long, 1862, Book 10, Section 6.

- The tennis elbow – thank you for encouraging me to practice moderation.

This kind of gratitude doesn't erase difficulty, but it changes your relationship with it. It stops you from fighting against reality. It allows you to move through challenges without wasting energy on resentment.

The Science of Gratitude

The Stoics knew that gratitude was powerful long before science caught up. And today, research confirms what they already practiced: gratitude is not just a mindset – it's a performance advantage.

Gratitude:

- Lowers stress and reduces anxiety.[32]
- Improves physical health by lowering inflammation.[33]
- Strengthens relationships and workplace culture.[34]

32   R McCraty & D Childre, *The Grateful Heart: The Psychophysiology of Appreciation*, HeartMath Research Center, Boulder Creek CA, 2004. *This study explores how feelings of gratitude and appreciation can reduce stress and anxiety by shifting heart rhythm patterns.*

33   R A Emmons & M E McCullough, 'Counting Blessings Versus Burdens: An Experimental Investigation of Gratitude and Subjective Well-Being in Daily Life', *Journal of Personality and Social Psychology*, vol. 84, no. 2, 2003, pp. 377–89. *This widely cited study shows how daily gratitude practices can improve overall well-being and reduce inflammatory markers over time.*

34   G A M Grant & F Gino, 'A Little Thanks Goes a Long Way: Explaining Why Gratitude Expressions Motivate Prosocial Behavior', *Journal of Personality and Social Psychology*, vol. 98, no. 6, 2010, pp. 946–55. *Their research demonstrates how gratitude strengthens social bonds and improves workplace relationships by increasing trust and cooperation.*

When practiced deliberately, gratitude functions as a psychological reset, shifting focus from what is lacking to what is valuable.

Every morning, when I put on my cochlear implant, I pause. I think about the scientists and doctors who made it possible for me to hear again. I think about the fact that I live in a time where this kind of technology exists. I think about how I couldn't socialise with the people I love – and now I can. I also reflect, often, on how this personal challenge has allowed me to experience just how mentally strong I am.

This moment of gratitude each morning shapes how I step into the day. It doesn't mean the day won't be difficult. It does mean I start with the right mindset.

Gratitude in Leadership

Gratitude isn't just personal – it changes how you lead others.

People perform better when they feel valued. Teams function better when appreciation is part of the culture. And leaders themselves stay clearer, more effective, and less burnt out when they *notice* what's working rather than just what needs fixing.

But real gratitude in leadership isn't just about saying *thank you* in an email. It's about presence. It's about actually seeing people and what they bring. It's about acknowledging effort, not just outcomes.

The difference between a leader who gets swallowed by frustration and a leader who navigates pressure with steadiness is often simply this: what they choose to see.

Making Gratitude a Habit (Without Overcomplicating it)

If gratitude is going to shape your mindset, it needs to be woven into your day – not as an extra task, but as a shift in awareness. One of the simplest ways to do this is by attaching gratitude to things you already do.

- While making coffee → Think of something you are grateful you *don't* have.
- Before a meeting → Take a moment to appreciate the people in the room.
- At the end of the day → Acknowledge one lesson, even if the day was hard.

None of this requires extra time. It's just about paying attention.

Over weeks and months, this shifts your baseline. You stop *trying* to be grateful and simply *are*.

Closing Reflection: THE CHOICE TO SEE CLEARLY

Gratitude isn't about pretending that everything is good. It's about refusing to be blind to what *is* good.

Life will always be uncertain. Work will always be demanding. There will always be setbacks, challenges, and moments of frustration. But the ability to choose gratitude, to find strength in appreciation even when the path is difficult, is always within our control.

This is why the Stoics valued gratitude so highly. Not because it made them *feel* better, but because it made them *see* better – not just in leadership, but in how we show up in every part of life.

GRATITUDE IN THE STRUGGLE

When I sat down with Renee, a Chief Operations Officer in the professional services sector, she began with what was taking up most of her energy – a colleague on her executive team who she was finding especially hard to work with.

> *'For months, I felt like I was dragging this person through every meeting. There was pushback on every decision, resistance to collaboration, and this constant undercurrent of tension.'*

At first, Renee tried to stay professional, hoping it would pass.

> *'But it wasn't passing. And I could feel myself getting worn down. I was starting to dread our interactions.'*

I asked what shifted.

> *'There was one meeting where they questioned me – again – on something I'd already explained. I snapped. Not out loud, but inside. I felt the anger rise. But instead of reacting, something in me*

paused. I heard my own internal voice say: This is a moment to step up.'

That pause gave her a new way to engage. She asked a genuine question – one that showed care and concern – and for the first time, really heard something different.

'I came to understand that, for my colleague, it wasn't about the project. It was about trust. About them feeling sidelined.'

That moment shifted something for them both.

'I realised I'd been so focused on how hard this person was making things for me, I hadn't stopped to ask what they were experiencing. That moment of frustration became a mirror. And oddly – a turning point.'

What emerged wasn't a sudden transformation, but a shift in how Renee approached the relationship.

'I started treating that dynamic as part of my leadership development. Every conversation became a chance to practise patience, perspective-taking, and staying anchored when I wanted to react. I'm not saying it was enjoyable. But it made me stronger.'

It's a common story with my clients. And like Renee, they often say:

'I wouldn't have chosen that dynamic. But I'm grateful for it. Because it made me more deliberate. Steadier. And a better leader than I was before.'

That's the quiet power of gratitude in leadership. It's not about feeling thankful for comfort or ease. It's about recognising the hard moments as part of the work – even a gift. Gratitude keeps us alert. It steadies us in the fire. And over time, it shapes us into leaders who are not only stronger – but wiser, and more human because of what we've faced.

Reflective Questions

Gratitude isn't just a feeling – it's a way of seeing. These questions help you move beyond surface-level gratitude and reconnect with what steadies you.

Pause and Notice

- What small moment today reminded me of what matters most?
- Who am I quietly grateful for – even if I haven't told them?
- What hard thing in my life is shaping me into someone wiser or more deliberate?

Lead with Gratitude

- How might I lead differently if I noticed what's working as often as I notice what's hard?
- What simple habit could help me stay anchored in gratitude – especially on the days that test me most?

Gratitude doesn't remove difficulty – but it changes how we meet it.

What's Next?

You've now completed *Part 1: Anchored Mindset* – the practices that steady you from the inside out.

Across these chapters, we've explored what it means to lead yourself well – especially when life doesn't go to plan.

You've reflected on life's impermanence (*Memento Mori*), embraced whatever comes (*Amor Fati*), learned to let go of what's outside your control, to shift perception, to strengthen emotional discipline, and to practise gratitude – not just when life is easy, but when it's hard.

These practices don't remove life's challenges – but they do steady you within them.

They are what ground you – so you can lead yourself, and others, well.

Now, we turn from mindset to action.

In *Part 2: Intentional Leadership*, we'll explore how anchored leaders move forward – how they act with clarity, courage, and care – not perfectly, but deliberately.

Anchored first. Intentional next.

PART 2

Intentional Action

The first part of this book focused on cultivating an anchored mindset – your inner foundation.

This next part moves from inner work to outer practice.

We'll explore what it means to act with courage and integrity, how to keep moving when progress is possible – and hold your nerve when it's not.

From anchored to intentional.

Chapter 9

THE FOUR VIRTUES OF STOIC LEADERSHIP – COURAGE, JUSTICE, TEMPERANCE, AND WISDOM

No man is free, who is not master of himself.

– EPICTETUS[35]

Leadership isn't for the faint-hearted. Every day, you make decisions that carry weight – shaping careers, influencing people's sense of purpose, and defining the culture of your team or organisation. You're expected to remain calm despite uncertainty, stay composed in crisis, and move forward without all the answers. The pressure doesn't let up.

And the toughest leadership battles? They aren't just external – they're internal.

---

35   Epictetus, *Discourses*, trans. E Carter, 1758, Book 2, Chapter 10, public domain.

How do you stay clear-headed in uncertainty? Make the right call when emotions run high? Keep your ego in check when success comes easily, and stay steady when setbacks hit hard?

The Stoics understood these challenges well. They knew that leadership isn't just about external success – it's about inner resolve. The ability to govern yourself before leading others.

At the heart of their philosophy were four essential virtues: Courage, Justice, Temperance, and Wisdom.

These aren't abstract ideals. They are practical disciplines – ways of thinking and acting that help you make better decisions, stay grounded under pressure, and lead with integrity when the stakes are high.

The Stoics saw these virtues as an ethical compass– guiding our thoughts, choices, and actions. And they recognised that each leader brings these virtues to life through their own personal values.

While the virtues are the foundation, personal values shape how they show up in practice – adapting to individual experiences, priorities, and leadership contexts.

For example, a leader who values innovation might express courage through bold decision-making. A leader who values community might show justice by ensuring everyone's voice is heard.

Personal values reflect what matters most to us – and the Stoic virtues help ensure we apply those values wisely, fairly, and with balance.

The virtues, then, are like the roots of a tree – universal and enduring – while personal values are the branches, shaped by individual experience but nourished by the same ethical foundation.

Let's explore how these core virtues connect to modern leadership – and how they work alongside your personal values to guide how you lead in practice.

COURAGE:
Facing Fear and Taking Action

Courage is the willingness to move forward even when fear is present.

Leadership requires courage every day – whether it's standing up for what's right, making an unpopular decision, or admitting when you're wrong. The fear of criticism, failure, or losing credibility can be paralysing. But avoiding hard decisions doesn't make them disappear – it only erodes trust.

I've seen this play out with leaders who've built their success by holding everything together – fixing problems, jumping into crises, proving their worth through sheer effort.

One leader I worked with hit that point. Burnout. Exhaustion. And the quiet realisation that his approach wasn't sustainable.

It took real courage to do something different – to step back, trust his team, and delegate. Not because it was easy, but because it was necessary.

For him, responsibility was everything. He valued being the person others could rely on. But once he embraced the Stoic view of courage – acting rightly despite fear – he realised that true responsibility wasn't about doing everything himself. It was about creating the conditions for others to step up and lead alongside him.

And that shift didn't just help him avoid burnout, it made him a better leader.

Courage is also about facing difficult moments head-on.

You may recall Tara, the leader we met in Chapter 7, responding to hours of technical questions during an external review. She understood the importance of self-regulation in moments of pressure – especially when the risk of being misinterpreted or saying the wrong thing felt high.

Instead of letting fear dictate her actions, she embraced a Stoic approach: she prepared rigorously, anticipated worst-case scenarios (*premeditatio malorum*[36]), and focused only on what she could control – her clarity, composure, and truthfulness. When the moment came, she handled it with steady determination.

Courageous leaders don't shift blame. They own their mistakes. They admit when they don't have the answers. And they lead by example.

As Seneca put it, 'It is not because things are difficult that we do not dare; it is because we do not dare that they are difficult.'[37]

---

36 *Premeditatio malorum* is a Stoic practice meaning 'premeditation of evils' – imagining what could go wrong in order to prepare calmly and respond with intention.
37 Seneca, Moral Letters to Lucilius, trans. R M Gummere, Loeb Classical Library, Harvard University Press, Cambridge, 1917, Letter 104, public domain.

But here's the nuance: while the virtue of courage is universal, how it shows up in practice depends on personal values.

A leader who values honesty might show courage by speaking uncomfortable truths. A leader who values collaboration might show it by facilitating difficult conversations.

The Stoic virtue provides the ethical backbone. Personal values shape its expression.

JUSTICE:
Doing What's Right, Not What's Easy

Justice in leadership isn't about rigid rule-following. It's about fairness, integrity, and ensuring that decisions serve the greater good – not personal gain, political convenience, or short-term fixes.

It's a challenge many leaders face when personal relationships and professional responsibility collide.

During a restructure, a leader I worked with found herself right in the middle of this tension. Some employees had become close friends over the years. Making objective decisions felt emotionally loaded.

But justice demanded fairness over familiarity. It meant making tough calls without favouritism – and ensuring transparency so that trust remained intact, even when the news was difficult.

Her personal values – compassion and loyalty – initially pulled her in another direction. She wanted to protect those she cared about.

But the Stoic virtue of justice didn't ask her to abandon compassion – it asked her to apply it fairly and without bias. By grounding her values in the framework of justice, she found clarity: compassion wasn't about shielding a few from discomfort – it was about ensuring everyone was treated with respect.

Justice demands that leaders rise above personal bias and short-term pressures.

Marcus Aurelius captured it best: 'What isn't good for the hive isn't good for the bee.'[38]

True leadership is about serving the collective good – not just the immediate or the personal.

TEMPERANCE:
Regulating Emotion and Maintaining Balance

Temperance is about self-regulation – knowing when to step in and when to hold back, when to speak and when to listen. It's what keeps leaders from burning out, lashing out, or making impulsive choices.

Many leaders I work with find themselves confronted by colleagues or clients with high emotions. The natural instinct is to match the intensity – to push back, argue, or defend. But the most skilful leaders do the opposite. They slow their breathing, lower their voice, and respond with steady composure.

---

38   M Aurelius, Meditations, adapted from the public domain translation by G Long, 1862, Book 6, Section 54.

The result? The conversation de-escalates, trust builds, and resolution comes faster than if they had reacted emotionally.

Temperance is also about setting boundaries. Early in their careers, many leaders pride themselves on being constantly available – late-night emails, back-to-back meetings, operating at full stretch. Over time, they come to realise it isn't sustainable. Their effectiveness suffers, and so does their judgment.

What shifts is the recognition that stepping away – pausing to reset, reflect, or recalibrate – isn't indulgent. It's a discipline. It makes them better decision-makers.

Personal values often shape how temperance shows up. For one leader, creativity was core – time spent in galleries wasn't a luxury; it was replenishment. For another, it was through their value of family – creating clear boundaries around evenings so they could be fully present with loved ones.

Temperance isn't just about restraint. It's about balance. Knowing when not to overreach, overreact, or overextend – and having the discipline to lead from that steadiness.

WISDOM:
Seeing the Bigger Picture

Wisdom is the ability to step back, assess situations clearly, and make sound decisions. Without it, leaders can get caught in short-term thinking – reacting impulsively, chasing quick wins, or allowing ego to drive their choices.

One of the most common ways this shows up is in how leaders manage their time and involvement.

It's a pattern I see often – leaders pulled into ongoing firefighting, working to stay across every detail, believing this is what strong leadership looks like. But over time, many come to realise that staying in the middle of everything doesn't build capability – it creates dependency.

This shift often comes through a hard-earned realisation: that wisdom isn't about having all the answers or being across every issue – it's about knowing when to step back. It's about trusting others, delegating effectively, and creating space for better thinking.

For many leaders, personal values like accountability initially drive this over-involvement. They believe that being in every conversation or solving every problem proves commitment. But Stoic wisdom offers a different perspective: real accountability isn't about doing it all – it's about creating the conditions for others to lead and succeed.

As Epictetus reminds us: 'No one can learn what they believe they already know.'[39]

Wise leaders cultivate curiosity and humility. They listen more than they speak. They challenge their own assumptions. They create space – for themselves and for their teams – to step back, reflect, and focus on what really matters.

Wisdom ties all the virtues together. It allows courage to be guided by good judgment, justice to be

---

39 *Epictetus, Discourses, trans. P E Matheson, 1916, Book 2, Chapter 17, public domain; adapted by the author..*

applied fairly, and temperance to be exercised with discernment. Without wisdom, boldness can turn into recklessness, fairness can become rigidity, and restraint can slip into passivity.

Wisdom gives us perspective – to act well, not just quickly. To see the bigger picture, not just the immediate problem. And to lead in a way that lasts.

Closing Reflection:
LEADERSHIP AS A JOURNEY OF CHARACTER

The four Stoic virtues – Courage, Justice, Temperance, and Wisdom – offer a steady foundation for leadership. They shape how you respond to fear, how you make decisions, how you regulate emotion, and how you stay focused on what matters most.

But they don't stand alone. These virtues guide how your personal values show up in practice – helping you lead in ways that are fair, thoughtful, and anchored in integrity.

If the Stoic virtues are the roots of steady leadership, your personal values are the branches – shaping your leadership style and guiding how you engage with the world around you. Whether you value integrity, compassion, achievement, or collaboration, the Stoic virtues help you stay grounded and balanced as you live those values out.

This is the work of leading well – built in action, shaped by small decisions, and practised in everyday moments; staying anchored in what matters. Choosing clarity over confusion, care over avoidance, and action over drift.

This is the work that shapes outcomes – and shapes you.

Rewriting the Rulebook –
LEADING THROUGH CRISIS

When I interviewed Jake – an executive leader of a major utility organisation – for this book, we started by talking about the four Stoic virtues: Courage, Justice, Temperance and Wisdom. What followed was one of the most powerful stories I'd heard about what it looks like to lead with character in a crisis.

Jake described standing inside an operations centre in late 2019, as devastating bushfires swept across parts of New South Wales and Victoria. He had just arrived in south-eastern New South Wales, where whole communities were under threat and critical services had been lost. Staff had taped together A3 printouts of a map to chart the damage based on reports radioed in by helicopters and calls from customers. They used highlighters to mark where key infrastructure had been lost. It quickly became clear that entire communities had been cut off from basic services.

The service network sprawled out like a spider web across the surrounding area. Pointing at the extremity of the spider web, Jake asked:

'How long will it be before we can resume services to these communities?'

The answer: 'Six weeks'.

That moment – what he now calls an epiphany – became a huge inflection point. Until then, the organisation's approach to natural disasters sat within its formal remit: to restore infrastructure. But something shifted for Jake. He could see that six weeks without critical services wasn't just an operational challenge – it was a human one.

'It hit me like a brick. We had to completely rethink what our role was in a disaster like this. Our job wasn't just to fix systems – it was to serve people. To support them through the six weeks they'd be without essential services. That was the real work.'

Jake picked up the phone and called a senior leader in customer experience. His message was clear:

'We need to flip our mindset. Fast.'

Within 24 hours, the organisation had sourced and delivered emergency equipment to affected communities. They assembled kits with essential items and built a simple app to coordinate the response. Teams began door-knocking the hardest-hit households, offering supplies and support packages, with a promise to return in 10 days to provide additional assistance.

The initiative wasn't part of any formal policy or emergency response plan. It was improvised. And controversial.

> *'I copped a lot of flak. Some people felt we were straying too far from our job. Others were worried we were pulling resources away from the technical recovery work. But we weren't. We used local staff who weren't involved in the rebuild. This was about service. Humanity.'*

What I heard in Jake's words wasn't just a logistical response. It was moral clarity. The kind of clarity that comes from the virtues we explored in Chapter 9:

- *Courage* to break away from the expected script, knowing there'd be pushback.
- *Justice* to do what is right for people, not just what is required by the rulebook.
- *Temperance* to stay balanced – redirecting resources wisely, without compromising core operations.
- *Wisdom* to see beyond immediate tasks and ask the bigger question: 'What do people really need from us right now?'

As Jake explained, as well as being about the genuine care for the community, it was also about building goodwill and creating space. By the time crews arrived to begin the rebuild, the temperature in those communities had shifted.

> *'Our teams weren't walking into streets full of angry customers. People had already been supported. They*

felt seen, heard. They were able to stay connected as a community. That changed everything.'

And it wasn't only those impacted who noticed.

'It built goodwill. Not just with the community, but with all key stakeholders. We weren't waiting for the questions – we were already doing the right thing.'

Since that moment, this broader, more human response has been embedded into every emergency the organisation has faced. Whether during storms, floods, or other crises, they now see their role not just as system rebuilders, but as community responders.

'We've gone into overdrive every time since, to support people in real ways. It gives us breathing space. And it's the right thing to do.'

Years later, when a well-respected industry consultant remarked, 'That wasn't your job.' Jake's response was clear:

'Maybe not. But I wouldn't change a thing.'

This story is a vivid illustration of Stoic leadership in practice: courage to act when the rules aren't enough, justice to put people at the centre, temperance to hold firm boundaries without becoming rigid, and wisdom to reframe the problem and respond with foresight.

Sometimes leadership requires stepping outside the lines, because the moment calls for more than just compliance.

It calls for character.

Reflective Questions

*These questions offer a way to reflect on the Stoic virtues
– courage, justice, temperance, and wisdom – and how
they show up in your leadership.*

Courage: Facing Fear and Taking Action

- Am I choosing what's right – or what's easy?
- What discomfort or uncertainty am
  I avoiding?
- When fear shows up, do I return to what's
  within my control?
- Do I lead by example when things are hard –
  or hold back until I feel certain?
- How do I respond when I make a mistake –
  do I own it or deflect?

Justice: Doing What's Right, Not What's Comfortable

- Am I treating all team members fairly,
  regardless of role or relationship?
- Do I listen openly before making decisions?
- Are my expectations clear, consistent, and
  reasonable?
- Have I created space for quieter voices or
  less represented perspectives?
- When mistakes happen, do I focus on
  learning – or blame?

Temperance: Regulating Emotion and Maintaining Balance

- Am I reacting emotionally – or responding with thoughtfulness?
- Do I have habits that help me recover, rest, and sustain energy?
- Have I set boundaries between work and personal life?
- In emotionally charged situations, do I pause before responding?
- Am I unconsciously rewarding overwork – in myself or others?

Wisdom: Seeing the Bigger Picture

- Am I making time to reflect, learn, and challenge my assumptions?
- Before acting, do I seek out different perspectives?
- Do I pause to consider long-term impact – not just immediate outcomes?
- Am I surrounding myself with people who challenge and expand my thinking?
- What lessons have I learned from recent challenges – and how will I apply them?

These aren't questions to tick off – they're ones to return to, especially when the noise of leadership gets loud.

What's Next?

The Stoic virtues remind us that leadership is built in action – shaped by what we stand for, how we show up, and the choices we make every day.

But living those virtues isn't a one-time decision. It's something we return to again and again – especially when progress is slow, results are uncertain, or setbacks arise.

That's where grit comes in.

Grit is what carries you through the long, unfinished work of leadership. It's the discipline to keep moving, to keep showing up – not perfectly, but persistently.

In the next chapter, we'll explore how leaders cultivate grit in action – and why staying in motion matters just as much as knowing where you stand.

Chapter 10

GRIT IN ACTION – STAYING IN MOTION WHEN IT MATTERS MOST

'Persist and resist.'

– EPICTETUS[40]

Wisdom helps us see the bigger picture, but leadership isn't just about knowing what matters – it's about taking action, especially when the path is unclear. And that's where grit comes in.

Some challenges test you immediately – you know exactly what needs to be done, and you act. Others wear you down over time. A tough quarter, a failing initiative, a leadership challenge that drags on longer than expected. Or maybe it's something more personal – recovering from a major setback, struggling with self-doubt, or navigating a situation where progress feels just out of reach.

---

40   Epictetus, *Discourses*, trans. E Carter, 1758, Book 1, Chapter 6, public domain.

This is something I see often in coaching. A leader comes to a session feeling stuck – not for lack of effort, but because progress has stalled. They've worked hard, refined their approach, sought input from others – and still, nothing seems to shift. It's frustrating. Doubt creeps in. They start questioning the project, the team, even themselves.

In those moments, what we explore together is how often momentum doesn't come from clarity first – it comes from action. Not a perfect solution. Not a grand fix. Just the next small, deliberate step. Something within their control.

Over time, that willingness to stay in motion – to keep showing up – begins to loosen the grip of self-doubt. Slowly, progress returns. And with it, confidence.

Grit isn't about blindly pushing through – it's about knowing when to persist, when to adapt, and when to let go. Stoicism teaches that while we can't control everything, we can always control how we respond. The leaders who thrive aren't necessarily the most talented or the most fortunate – they are the ones who take deliberate action, even when the path is unclear.

Grit is the discipline to keep showing up. It's the practice of forward motion – of doing the next small thing, even when motivation runs low and certainty is missing. It's the commitment to keep going when the easy choice would be to stop.

The Discipline of Taking Action

The easiest trap to fall into is overthinking and inaction. You might hesitate because you're unsure of the right step, afraid of making a mistake, or waiting for perfect conditions. But progress doesn't come from knowing what to do – it comes from doing it.

This is something clients often bring to coaching. They share that they're caught in a loop of over-analysis – running endless scenarios, seeking more data, and debating every option –without actually moving forward. It can feel exhausting and frustrating, especially when the pressure to get it right is high.

What we often explore together is the shift from seeking perfect answers to taking intentional action. Instead of waiting for full clarity, they begin to understand that clarity can be created through movement. Focusing on the next best step – rather than the ideal one – often unlocks momentum. And with that small shift, confidence grows, and decisions start to come with more ease.

James Clear, in *Atomic Habits*[41], reinforces this idea: meaningful progress doesn't come from sudden breakthroughs but from small, deliberate actions repeated consistently over time. Taking action – no matter how small – creates momentum, and momentum builds confidence.

There's another pattern I see with senior leaders – especially after a public setback or a decision that didn't land well. It can rattle their sense of self. Suddenly,

---

41   Clear, *Atomic Habits*, 2018.

they find themselves hesitating. Pulling back. Second-guessing their judgement – not because they don't know what to do, but because the sting of past failure is still fresh.

What I often say in those moments is: courage isn't about eliminating fear. It's about choosing to act alongside it.

For many leaders, the turning point isn't dramatic. It starts small – with a project they care about but have been avoiding. A quiet re-entry into work that feels meaningful. And from that small action comes connection. From connection comes momentum. Eventually, their sense of self returns – not because the fear disappeared, but because they remembered what it felt like to move forward again.

As one client told me, 'I realised I was waiting for certainty I'd never get. But once I started acting again, I remembered who I was. Action restored my confidence.'

That's grit too – not just persistence, but recovery. The choice to re-enter the arena after doubt, to step forward when staying safe would be easier.

Epictetus' advice – 'Persist and resist.'[42] – captures the essence of Stoic grit. Persist in what matters. Resist distractions, fear, and inaction.

---

42   Epictetus, *Discourses* (Carter, 1758), Book 1, Chapter 6.

Humility and the Strength in Letting Go

Stoicism teaches that ego is the enemy of adaptability. As Epictetus observed, 'No one can learn what they believe they already know.'[43] Grit without humility can easily become tunnel vision. But humility strengthens grit by keeping it grounded, reflective, and open to growth.

Great leaders understand that humility isn't doubt – it's the confidence to stay curious, open, and to step back when it helps others thrive. The strongest leaders recognise that humility is a quiet strength – rooted in curiosity, openness, and the ability to create space for others to contribute and grow.

A common theme that shows up in coaching is the tension leaders feel around delegation. Many are incredibly capable and deeply committed to their teams – but they carry a strong sense of responsibility to have the answers. Even when they trust their people, they can feel the weight of needing to lead from certainty.

Over time, what often emerges in coaching is a realisation: leadership isn't about knowing it all – it's about creating the conditions for great thinking to surface.

This shift – from offering quick solutions to asking thoughtful questions – is a powerful form of grit. It takes patience, emotional discipline, and trust. When leaders let go of perfectionism and embrace progress as an iterative process, they discover a new kind of

---

43   Epictetus, *Discourses*, trans. P E Matheson, 1916, Book 2, Chapter 17, public domain; adapted by the author.

strength: one rooted not in control, but in collective progress.

The result? More engaged, confident teams – and leaders who are more effective because they're willing to listen, learn, and adapt.

Marcus Aurelius reminds us: 'Be understanding with others, and disciplined with yourself.'[44] This means setting high standards for yourself while recognising that leadership is not about control – it's about guiding others through challenges with clarity and composure.

Closing Reflection:
GRIT AS A LEADERSHIP LEGACY

Grit is not just about pushing through obstacles – it's about staying in motion with purpose. The best leaders don't simply persist for the sake of it; they persist in what matters and adapt when necessary.

As a leader, your ability to model determination shapes the culture around you. Your response to setbacks, uncertainty, and challenges teaches your team how to navigate difficulty – not with blind determination, but with thoughtful action. Grit is not about forcing progress. It's about knowing when to push forward, when to pivot, and when to pause.

However, even the strongest leaders will face moments when persistence isn't enough – when the challenge is greater than sheer willpower, when

---

44   M Aurelius, *Meditations*, adapted from the public domain translation by G Long, 1862, Book 5, Section 33.

circumstances refuse to bend, and when exhaustion starts to take its toll.

This is where grit meets its edge – and fortitude begins. The next chapter will take us there.

WHEN GRIT MEETS GRACE

This is a personal story a client shared with me in a coaching session – and it hit home for me, especially as a parent. I've worked with many leaders who thrive on logic. That mindset works well in professional environments – until you meet a five-year-old at bedtime. Suddenly, everything you thought you knew about leadership gets redefined. I've heard versions of this story from many clients over the years, so I'm sharing it here.

> *'I used to think persistence was about brute force – about pushing through obstacles with sheer will. But life has a way of teaching lessons in unexpected ways. If you'd told me ten years ago that the greatest lesson in grit would come not from work, but from bedtime battles with my son, I would have laughed.'*

What began as a seemingly small challenge quickly became a nightly test of endurance.

> *'Teeth brushing? A war zone. Pyjamas? A negotiation that would put high-stakes mergers to shame. And sleep? Forget it.'*

ANCHORED AND INTENTIONAL

Like many capable leaders I coach, this client brought a structured, outcome-focused mindset to the problem. They tried everything – parenting books, reward systems, clear boundaries.

> *'I tried different methods, different tones, different incentives. Nothing worked. Every night felt like a defeat.'*

In our conversation, they described the night everything started to shift. After a particularly gruelling day – dealing with a major setback at work – they came home exhausted, only to find themselves in a familiar bedtime battle.

> *'My son was wired, overtired, and defiant. I felt my patience snap. My voice rose –louder than I intended. He froze, his face crumpled, and I felt like I'd failed.*
>
> *I walked out for a moment, and sat in the hallway, my head in my hands. I had spent the entire day negotiating with executives, staying composed in high-pressure situations, and yet here I was, losing my cool over pyjamas.'*

Something shifted in that moment. As we reflected on it together, we explored one of the central ideas from this chapter: grit isn't just about pushing forward. It's about choosing how to show up when you're tired, discouraged, or unsure.

> *'The real battle wasn't about getting my son to sleep. It was about how I showed up, even when I was exhausted.'*

That night, he tried something different. He stopped pushing and started listening.

'My son told me about a bad dream he'd had the night before. We talked about it. I sat with him until he felt safe.'

It didn't change overnight. It took weeks of experimenting, getting it wrong, adjusting, and trying again. But eventually, things shifted.

'The bedtime battles stopped being battles. I reframed them as moments, and took them one moment at a time.'

In coaching, we linked this to a broader insight: grit is about staying in motion – but it also requires humility to adapt.

Their story illustrated so many of the grit themes we explored in this chapter – small, consistent steps; choosing action over perfection; and showing up, especially when it's hard.

Sometimes, grit means pushing forward. Other times, it means stepping back or sideways, listening, and staying with the discomfort long enough to understand what needs to change.

And sometimes, the biggest lessons come not from work or books – but from a tired five-year-old who just needs to feel safe enough to sleep.

This was a story about parenting. About leadership. And about presence. Mostly, it was about the power of returning, again and again, to what matters most.

Reflective Questions:

Grit isn't about force. It's about focus. It's about staying in motion – even when progress is slow, unseen, or uncertain.

- Where in my work or life have I been waiting for clarity, when what I really need is to take action?
- What's one small step I could take this week to build momentum?
- Am I holding back, waiting for perfect conditions – or am I willing to act with what I know now?
- How do I respond when progress stalls – do I push harder, pause, or pull back?
- When have I let fear of failure or past mistakes stop me from trying again?
- Where do I need to bring more humility – letting go of control so others can step up?
- What practice helps me reconnect with what matters most when I'm tired, discouraged, or uncertain?

Grit is built in the doing – step by step, choice by choice. Start small. Keep moving.

What's Next?

There are times when even your most determined effort doesn't move the dial. When persistence meets an unmovable wall. When the work isn't about pushing ahead – but about holding still.

That's where fortitude steps in.

While grit helps you stay in motion, fortitude helps you stand firm. Grit keeps you moving when the path is unclear. Fortitude gives you the strength to stand firm when there's no clear path at all.

Both require courage. But fortitude emerges when the work demands more than action. It calls for presence, patience, and inner resolve.

In the next chapter, we'll explore fortitude as the quiet power that sustains leaders through adversity. Because leadership isn't always about moving forward. Sometimes, it's about holding your ground until the storm passes.

Chapter 11

FLOATING WITH THE TIDE – THE POWER OF FORTITUDE

Make the best use of what is in your power, and take the rest as it happens.

– EPICTETUS[45]

Clear thinking, determination, and decisive action are essential, but they are not always enough. Some challenges cannot be resolved, no matter how much grit you apply or how relentlessly you stay in motion. At times, persistence alone won't break through the barriers in front of you.

And these moments, when effort does not yield results, are a true test of character.

This is when we must learn to dig deep – to endure, and to hold steady even when life has us by the throat.

---

45 Epictetus, Enchiridion, trans. E Carter, 1758, Section 1, public domain.

This is fortitude.

Fortitude is what remains when action is no longer effective. It's the quiet strength to hold your ground when momentum has stalled, and no next step is clear. When you've done all you can and progress still eludes you, fortitude is the force that steadies you in the uncertainty and reminds you that not all growth is immediate or visible.

Beyond Persistence

In the previous chapter, we explored persistence – the ability to keep taking action despite obstacles, adjusting as necessary, and staying in motion even when progress feels slow. Persistence is proactive and deliberate; it's about making choices, responding to setbacks with clarity, and refusing to be derailed by difficulty.

But fortitude is something different. It begins when action is no longer possible. It's not about pushing forward – it's about holding your ground when there's no clear next move. Where persistence moves, fortitude remains. It is the ability to remain grounded when everything around you feels uncertain or out of control.

And fortitude often begins with accepting an uncomfortable truth: you may never have the full picture. Life events, leadership decisions, and personal challenges rarely arrive with all the puzzle pieces in view. There's often something just out of sight, a factor you only learn in hindsight. Fortitude is the ability to endure without those answers – to keep breathing through uncertainty and hold steady, even when the crowd is pulling you in another direction.

Going With the Tide vs. Swimming for Shore

Hunter S. Thompson, an American journalist and author, is often credited with the idea: Who is the happier man, he who has braved the storm of life and lived or he who has stayed securely on shore and merely existed?

There will be moments in life and leadership when braving the storm is necessary – when the right move is to take action, to fight, to push forward. But there will also be times when you must stop resisting and go with the tide, trusting that letting go and staying afloat is, for now, enough.

As Thompson also observed: 'That is the question – whether to float with the tide, or to swim for a goal. It is a choice we must all make.'[46]

We are often taught that persistence is the only way to succeed. But fortitude is different. It is not about always swimming toward the shore at full force. Sometimes, the wisest decision is to conserve energy, toughen your resolve, and dig in until conditions change.

---

46   H S Thompson, letter to Hume Logan, 1958, in *Letters of Note: Correspondence Deserving of a Wider Audience*, compiled by S Usher, Canongate Books, Edinburgh, 2013.

The strongest leaders don't just push forward; they know when to hold steady and accept things as they are.

It's a lesson many leaders face at some point – the moment when effort isn't enough, and acceptance is the only way forward.

One senior leader shared how this tested them more than any technical challenge they'd faced. They had spent years building a division from the ground up – leading with energy, creativity, and relentless effort. But then the market shifted. Budgets were cut. Decisions came down from above that were out of their hands.

'I kept thinking there had to be a way to fix it,' they told me. 'I tried everything – reframing the strategy, finding alternative funding, making the case to leadership. But it was over.'

What stayed with me was what they said next.

'It took everything in me to accept it. I had to stop fighting. I had to stand firm in the storm, knowing I had done everything I could – and trust that letting go wasn't giving up. It was what the moment asked of me.'

That's fortitude.

It's not about surrendering your standards or ambition. It's about recognising when the work shifts – from action to endurance. From driving forward to holding steady. From control to acceptance.

Even when we fail, or face our deepest and most gut-wrenching challenges, we can learn to accept it for what it is. Then we can adapt for the next time and strengthen our resolve. And that is the gift of fortitude, if we choose to see it as such.

When all else has failed, we can still grow – for the next time.

Keep Showing Up

Fortitude often feels like fear. People mistake fear for weakness, when in fact, it is the emotional backdrop of courage. As one client put it:

'Bravery feels like fear. Because it is. They coexist. When I stepped into my new role, I was terrified every day. But I kept showing up despite the fear, and I came to realise I was actually being brave. I'd tell myself: show up, be a good person, look after people, make the right decisions, and show up and do the same again tomorrow. It was incredibly freeing when I realised my fear wasn't proof of failure – it was proof of bravery.'

My client didn't wait for the fear to subside. They simply showed up, day after day, which led to a shift in their perspective, and bravery followed.

Another client reflected on how this mindset shaped their approach to leadership – and life:

'One thing I've always believed, in all areas of life, not just work, is that sometimes the hardest part of success is just showing up. When you see athletes at the start line of the Olympics, they've already won in a way. They've done the training, avoided injury, and shown up every single day. That's victory. Whatever success I've had, it's come down to that – showing up, not just walking through the door, but being fully present, trying every day, and taking the right actions for the right reasons.'

This client highlights an intentional approach – a willingness to show up with self-agency, even when certainty is out of reach.

This is what fortitude looks like in practice – not grand declarations, but the steady resolve to return each day with intention, even when the outcome remains uncertain. To hold steady, even when fear whispers you're not enough.

Fortitude doesn't erase fear; it exists alongside it, reminding you of your inner resolve and the quiet victory that comes from standing firm, one day at a time.

Self-Determination – Your Choice

As Epictetus reminds us, 'Men are disturbed not by things, but by the view which they take of them.'[47]

This is where all the principles we've covered come together:

- *Memento Mori* – remember that life is fleeting.
- *Amor Fati* – embrace your fate rather than resist it. Accept that hardship is shaping you.
- Let go of control – recognise what is within your power and release what is not.
- Manage perception – choose a perspective that serves you.
- Use reason – don't let emotions cloud your judgment.
- Express gratitude – even in difficulty, there is something to be learned.

---

47   Epictetus, *Enchiridion*, trans. E Carter, 1758, Section 5, public domain.

- Use the four virtues as a compass – courage, justice, temperance, and wisdom.
- Grit in action – recognise how purposeful persistence moves you forward.

When nothing is working and fortitude is needed, these Stoic principles become the foundation that allows us to endure. Because fortitude isn't about blind endurance – it's about self-determination. It's the quiet but powerful reminder that you always have a choice. You can stay, or you can leave. You can fight, or you can let go. As the Stoics remind us, while we can't always control our circumstances, we can always control how we perceive them and the choices we make in response.

The power lies in choosing consciously and deliberately, rather than feeling pushed by circumstance.

This mindset – of consciously choosing how we show up – is something I hear often in coaching conversations. It sounds simple in theory, but it's incredibly powerful in practice. One client shared how this shift helped him navigate a particularly intense period at work – not by changing the situation, but by changing how he met it. As he described to me:

'I keep coming back to this thought: I'm fortunate to be here. We're going through a crazy period – big projects landing, the usual dramas – but I remember sitting on the train last week, saying to myself: I chose this. I choose to do this role. I choose to be in this position. I choose to deal with this craziness. And as soon as I reminded myself that it was my decision, I felt back in control.'

That practice – noticing his internal narrative and deliberately shifting it – became a steadying force.

'Of course, the next step is to follow that up: Okay, now you've made the choice, so work through it. My actions, my behaviour, my choices – showing up and getting on with it. In tough moments, that's what steadies me: this was my decision, my choice. That reminder allows me to refocus and feel more grounded.'

We talked about how this wasn't about false positivity or ignoring difficulty. It was about perspective – meeting reality with clarity and ownership.

And it shaped how he led others too: 'I speak to myself the way I'd speak to someone I care about – clear, honest, and compassionate. And I apply that same approach with my team. Clear is kind. Unclear is unkind[48]. It's true for how I lead others, but it's just as true for how I lead myself.'

This kind of self-talk – clear, steady, kind – is a skill. And like all skills, it's built through practice. As he summed it up to me: 'At the end of the day, I have a choice – about my role, my workplace, my path. And if I'm choosing to stay, I need to stop feeling sorry for myself and focus on what I can control. Show up, make the best decisions I can with the information I have, and keep going.'

That's what I see in leaders who stay grounded under pressure. They don't deny that it's hard. They don't try to control the uncontrollable. But they do

---

48   B Brown, *Dare to Lead: Brave Work. Tough Conversations. Whole Hearts.*, Random House, New York, 2018.

choose their perspective. They stay anchored in what matters most to them – their values, their actions, their way of showing up – and they keep moving forward.

Not because it's easy.

But because they've chosen to.

And that's what fortitude really is: not just endurance for endurance's sake, but the conscious choice to face challenges with clarity, grounded in the principles that steady us when nothing else does.

Anchoring Yourself in What Matters

Fortitude requires clarity about *why* you're enduring. Without this, the emotional toll can lead to burnout.

When the weight of uncertainty bears down on you, anchoring yourself in your core values and a clear sense of purpose becomes your steadfast compass.

One client shared how his parents' unwavering commitment to his education and early life instilled in him a deep appreciation for endurance. He explained: 'They got me to the starting line, and it would be poor form to waste that – and now I want to do the same for my children.'

In these moments, fortitude emerges from the heart – a grounded determination that propels you forward.

Another described how reconnecting to purpose helped them endure with intention: 'At times, I've been really challenged by the work, questioning: Why am I here? What is my purpose? I remind myself that I'm here for my team and for our clients. There always has to be a purpose that I'm aligned with.'

Ultimately, when you root your actions in what truly matters – your values, purpose, and commitment to others – as well as yourself – these become the anchors that keep you steady in times of fortitude.

Leading Well Means Leaning Well

One of the things I often explore with clients is this simple but important reminder: fortitude isn't isolation. Yes, it's about inner strength – but it's also about knowing when to lean on others. I say this often in coaching sessions because I see how easy it is for leaders to slip into the belief that they have to hold everything together, alone.

Sometimes, the most powerful thing I can offer as a coach is validation – meeting someone's experience without minimising it or rushing to fix it. One client described how simply being met with presence and patience during a tough time brought unexpected relief. They didn't need fixing. They just needed to feel seen, heard, and validated. That's often what fortitude looks like in practice: not a solo effort, but a shared one. The ability to lean – even briefly – can restore the strength to stand.

For another client, it wasn't conversation that helped – it was perspective. I often encourage leaders to widen their lens, to seek out stories and voices beyond their immediate world. Books, podcasts, conversations with people who've walked a similar path – these things offer more than advice. They offer proof that endurance is possible.

As one of them shared: 'Hearing how other people navigated the same kind of challenge helped me see my situation differently. It didn't make the problem disappear, but it felt like proof that I'd come out the other side.'

And support doesn't always come from people. Several of the leaders I work with find their steadiness in solitude – in movement, nature, or stillness. One described their practice this way: 'When everything felt overwhelming, I'd go for a run. That's when my mind would settle, and I'd remember: I've faced hard things before. I'll get through this, too.'

This is the work of fortitude – not withdrawing or pretending to be invincible, but knowing what holds you up and reaching for it without apology. Sometimes it's a conversation. Sometimes it's movement or stillness. Sometimes it's simply being seen and heard.

Whatever form it takes, I often ask leaders: 'What replenishes you? Who helps you feel more like yourself? Where do you turn when the load gets heavy?'

Fortitude isn't about carrying everything alone.

It's about knowing when to ask for help – and recognising that reaching out isn't a sign you're not coping. It's often the smartest, most human thing you can do.

Closing Reflection:
THE QUIET STRENGTH
OF FORTITUDE

Fortitude is not loud. It does not shout or fight for attention. It is the quiet strength of standing firm when there is no immediate way forward. It is the ability to endure what must be endured without losing yourself in the process.

Even when we fail, we can learn. We can adapt for the next time. In fact, it's the moments of failure and adversity that offer the greatest opportunity to experience that steely inside. Comfort doesn't call for it. Your darkest and most challenging moments do.

This takes practice, strength, and steadiness.

It takes fortitude.

Because in the end, this too shall pass. And when it does, you will be stronger for it. And ready for whatever comes next.

Steely Inside –
A STORY OF FORTITUDE

When I interviewed my executive client, Alannah, for the book, I was struck by how her story brought the themes of fortitude to life – not as a grand, heroic act, but as a deeply human, quiet strength. In coaching,

I often hear leaders talk about those pivotal moments of choice: to stay or go, to hold on or let go, to push through or step back. Alannah's story is one of those moments – a real-life example of what it means to float with the tide when swimming for shore isn't an option.

> *'I never expected to find myself at the centre of a leadership upheaval. One day, everything was relatively stable – the next, our organisation was thrown into turmoil. Our CEO was suddenly replaced, and the person stepping in couldn't have been more different. It wasn't just a shift in leadership style; it was a cultural mismatch.'*

As we talked, Alannah described how quickly the ripple effect spread. Trust was shaken. Long-standing leaders began to leave. The culture they had worked so hard to build started to unravel.

> *'I had a choice, like everyone else. Walk away, or stay and navigate the storm. I chose to stay. Not because I couldn't leave, but because I didn't want to. I cared about what we'd built, and I wasn't ready to walk away without seeing it through. But staying demanded something more than grit – it demanded fortitude.'*

This distinction matters. As we explored together, grit is about action – about staying in motion. Fortitude is about remaining steady when there's no clear next move – when the only thing you *can* control is your own response.

I asked where that kind of fortitude comes from, and like many leaders I work with, Alannah traced it back to an early formative experience.

> 'For me, it goes way back – to when I was fourteen and diagnosed with a health condition that changed everything. There was no choice, no negotiation. It was happening, and I had to deal with it. I remember thinking, Well, what's the alternative? I'm certainly not going to let this thing get me. That mindset – that inner strength – became part of who I am.'

This inner steel – quiet, anchored, deeply personal – was exactly what steadied Alannah through the upheaval.

> 'There were days when the situation felt absurd, when decisions made no sense and the noise from the press, the board, and the wider industry was deafening. But I kept coming back to one thing: I have to live with myself at the end of this.'

That reflection echoed a theme I see often in coaching – the role of self-determination in fortitude. You can't control the storm around you, but you can stay anchored in who you are.

> 'People think it's about dramatic stands, but it's not. It's the small, stubborn refusal to let the situation win. I remember telling my team, "What we had is gone. No decision we make today will bring it back. So let's focus on what's in front of us and make the best of it." That wasn't giving up – it was realism.

Fortitude is knowing when to stop fighting for what was and start working with what is."

We also reflected on uncertainty – a constant companion in leadership.

'Fortitude is about being able to sit with uncertainty without letting it erode your sense of self. You trust your gut, make the best decisions with the information you have, and stay true to your values.'

Those values were her anchor through the storm.

'Fortitude isn't just about endurance – it's about how you endure. For me, that meant treating people fairly, making choices I could stand by, and refusing to let frustration push me into actions that didn't align with who I wanted to be.'

And like many leaders I coach, my client spoke about the importance of support – not as weakness, but as wisdom.

'Fortitude doesn't mean isolation. It means surrounding yourself with people who can hold you up when you're running low. I remember a coaching session during that time. I shared something that, on the surface, might have seemed small. But it didn't feel small to me. My coach didn't brush it off or try to rationalise it. Instead, she met my frustration with the same weight I was feeling. That moment – being understood without having to justify myself – was like someone taking a load off my back.'

We also talked about the cumulative effect of small moments – the offhand comment, the overlooked contribution, the missed communication. It's often these that test fortitude the most.

> 'They build up, quietly chipping away at your resolve. If you're not paying attention, it's one of those small things – not the big crises – that can tip you over the edge.'

Looking back, Alannah described fortitude as a quiet, stubborn belief that while you can't control the world around you, you can control how you respond.

> 'It's knowing yourself well enough to understand what you can take on, when you need help, and when it's time to step away. It's acting with courage to face the unknown and justice to do what feels right. It's about being steely inside – not hard, not unyielding, but quietly, powerfully anchored in the one thing you can control: yourself.'

That's what fortitude in leadership looks like – not loud or dramatic, but found in the quiet discipline of staying grounded, staying true to yourself, and staying in it for as long as it takes.

Reflective Questions:

Fortitude isn't built overnight. It's shaped by the choices we make in hard seasons – and by how we steady ourselves for whatever comes next. It's not about doing more. It's about holding your ground, staying anchored in what matters, and showing up with quiet determination.

Take a moment to reflect:

- When have I faced a situation where effort alone wasn't enough? What helped me endure?
- What values or principles anchor me when I'm under pressure?
- Where in my leadership am I holding on too tightly – when acceptance might serve me better?
- What does *showing up* look like for me – even on the hard days?
- Who or what helps replenish me when I feel like I'm running low?
- How can I remind myself that asking for help is a strength, not a weakness?
- What do I want to carry forward from a past challenge – for the next time I face difficulty?

Fortitude isn't about waiting for life to get easier – it's about becoming steadier for whatever comes next.

What's Next?

Anchored thinking. Intentional action.

This is the rhythm of steady leadership.

The final part of this book is designed to help you stay with that practice – not in theory, but in the small, everyday choices that shape who you are and how you lead.

Fifty-two, weekly, reflections. A space to pause. To check in with yourself. To reconnect with what matters most.

Not to add pressure – but to offer perspective.

A way to stay anchored.

A way to lead with intention.

PART 3

Staying On Track – Weekly Reflections For Leadership Practice

Marcus Aurelius, emperor of Rome and the most powerful man of his time, lived nearly 2,000 years ago. Yet, when you read his private journal, Meditations, it's striking how familiar his struggles feel. He faced uncertainty, criticism, exhaustion, competing priorities, and the constant tension between personal well-being and professional responsibility. Sound familiar?

Leadership, it seems, has always been a balancing act – regardless of status, era, or circumstance.

What's even more striking is that, despite the weight of running an empire, Marcus still made time to write, reflect, and work on himself. He didn't do it because he was drowning or doubting his abilities. He did it because he knew self-reflection wasn't a luxury – it was what kept him steady, focused, and intentional. If someone with that level of responsibility could pause and think things through, it's a reminder that we all can. And probably should.

The reflections that follow are drawn from coaching conversations with my clients. They're simplified and anonymised but shared with a clear purpose: to show how ancient Stoic principles can support real people facing real challenges today – people who are committed to staying grounded and deliberate in how they lead.

You'll notice these aren't grand, sweeping transformations. They're small mindset shifts, daily choices, and moments of clarity that quietly reshape how someone leads and lives. As you read, I invite you to reflect on your own experiences.

Which stories feel familiar? Where might a shift in perspective – like Marcus Aurelius often reminded himself – help you move through challenges with more calm and clarity?

These examples aren't answers. They're here to spark your own reflections and show how the Stoic ideas in this book might offer steadiness and support, not just when times are tough, but in the everyday practice of being an anchored and intentional leader.

Week 1
MEMENTO MORI

'Waste no more time arguing about what a good
man should be. Be one.'

– MARCUS AURELIUS[49]

Where are you overthinking – when it's time to
take action?

Coaching Moment

Sam, a senior leader, had been stuck on a difficult team
decision for weeks. He was overthinking every angle –
trying to find the perfect words, the perfect timing, the
perfect solution.

'I've replayed how to say it over and over,' Sam told
me. 'I just don't want to get it wrong.'

We talked about how aiming for perfect can quietly
turn into avoiding. Instead, we focused on what sort of
leader Sam chose to be: honest, steady, and respectful.
Not necessarily perfect – but always genuine.

Sam took the next team meeting as their moment –
sharing the outcome openly and clearly, acknowledging
it might be difficult to hear.

Later Sam reflected, 'What surprised me most was
how the team responded. They appreciated the honesty.
They could see I wasn't just delivering an outcome – I
was showing care for them in how I handled it.'

---

49   M Aurelius, *Meditations*, adapted from the public domain
translation by G Long, 1862, Book 10, Section 16.

Week 2
ILLUSION OF CONTROL

'You have power over your mind – not outside events. Realise this, and you will find strength.'

–MARCUS AURELIUS[50]

Reflect on situations where you've felt out of control. How can focusing on your internal responses change your experience?

Coaching Moment

Camille, a senior leader navigating an organisational restructure, came into a coaching session visibly tense. She described how decisions were being made above her level, impacting her team without warning. 'It's exhausting,' Camille said, 'feeling like everything's shifting under my feet, and I can't do a thing about it.'

We talked about the Stoic idea of control – the difference between external events and internal responses. Camille questioned, 'What if, instead of trying to control the restructure, I focus only on how I show up in the middle of it?'

Camille decided to experiment. In meetings, she focused on staying calm and clear, asking thoughtful questions rather than reacting to news she couldn't change. With her team, Camille doubled down on what was within reach: setting priorities, maintaining trust, and offering reassurance without overpromising.

---

50   M Aurelius, *Meditations* (Long, 1862).

A few weeks later, Camille shared how things had shifted – not externally, but internally. 'The restructure's still messy, but I'm not riding the emotional rollercoaster anymore. I'm clear on what's mine to influence and what's not.'

Week 3
MEMENTO MORI

'When you arise in the morning, think of what a
precious privilege it is to be alive—to breathe, to
think, to enjoy, to love.'

– MARCUS AURELIUS[51]

Begin each day with gratitude. How does
acknowledging the simple privileges of life influence
your leadership?

Coaching Moment

Taylor, a senior manager leading a high-pressure
project, often started the day with a jolt of anxiety –
emails, deadlines, and urgent meetings filling their
mind before even stepping out of bed. During one
of our sessions, Taylor reflected, 'I wake up already
bracing for the day. It's like I'm running a race I didn't
sign up for.'

We explored how a Stoic-inspired morning
practice might change that. Taylor decided to start each
day with a short pause – three slow breaths, followed by
silently acknowledging three simple privileges: waking
up healthy, having work that mattered, and the people
she cared about.

A week later, Taylor described the shift: 'It didn't
make the workload smaller, but I stopped feeling

---

51   Adapted from M Aurelius, *Meditations*, public domain sources
including Book 8, Section 36.

like the day was attacking me. I walked into my first meeting already anchored, not flustered.' Even her team noticed. 'You seem calmer,' one colleague mentioned after a typically tense project update.

Taylor realised that gratitude didn't erase challenges, but it did shape how she approached them: 'When you start the day appreciating life itself, the noise loses its grip. I'm leading from a steadier place now.'

Week 4
PERCEPTION

'The happiness of your life is shaped by the
quality of your thoughts.'

– MARCUS AURELIUS[52]

Monitor your thought patterns this week. What
negative thoughts can you reframe to improve your
well-being and leadership?

Coaching Moment

Catherine, a department lead, was stuck in a cycle
of frustration. 'I keep thinking the team's too slow,'
she told me. 'It's draining me – and I'm getting short
with people.'

We explored how thought patterns shape our
reactions. I asked, 'What happens if you reframe it?
Instead of 'they're slow,' could it be 'they're being
thorough'?'

Catherine paused. 'But what if they are being slow?'

Then the question becomes less about judgement –
and more about clear expectations and action. 'What's
getting in the way? How can I help clear a path?'

That shift changed everything. 'I didn't realise how
much I was fuelling my own frustration,' Catherine said.
'Now I'm not reacting – I'm asking better questions.'

---

52   M Aurelius, Meditations, adapted from the public domain
translation by G Long, 1862, Book 5, Section 16.

Week 5

THE FOUR STOIC VIRTUES

'If it is not right, do not do it; if it is not true, do
not say it.'

– MARCUS AURELIUS[53]

Assess your decisions and communications. Are they
aligned with your values?

Coaching Moment

Claire, an executive overseeing a high-stakes project,
faced pressure to present progress in an overly optimistic
light. 'The board wants reassurance,' she explained. 'I'm
tempted to downplay the risks, but it doesn't sit right.'

Reflecting on the Stoic virtues, and her personal
values of trust and honesty, Claire decided to hold firm.
She presented the situation clearly – acknowledging
progress while highlighting risks without dramatising
them. 'It felt risky in the moment,' she later admitted,
'but the response surprised me. They appreciated the
honesty and asked how they could help.'

For Claire, this became a leadership touchstone:
'I'd rather face a tough conversation with integrity than
smooth things over and lose credibility.'

---

53   M Aurelius, *Meditations*, trans. G Long, 1862, Book 12, Section 17,
public domain.

Week 6
FORTITUDE

'The best revenge is not to be like your enemy.'

– MARCUS AURELIUS[54]

When wronged, consider how maintaining your integrity serves as the best response.

Coaching Moment

Sam, a senior leader, felt attacked by a peer in an Executive team meeting. 'My first instinct was to hit back – to point out their own failures,' Sam admitted.

Having worked hard on emotional regulation, Sam chose a different approach. He took a breath and told himself to remain calm, he asked clarifying questions to demonstrate open-mindedness, while also advocating for his perspective.

'It wasn't easy,' Sam reflected, 'but I realised the moment I matched their behaviour, I'd lose sight of my own standards.' A week later, the same colleague approached him privately, conceding they'd acted out of frustration.

'Integrity,' Sam concluded, 'isn't just about feeling good about yourself. It's about staying steady and giving others the space to do the same.'

---

54   M Aurelius, *Meditations*, trans. G Long, 1862, Book 6, Section 6, public domain.

Week 7

MEMENTO MORI

'It's not death that should frighten us, but the
fear of never truly living.'

– MARCUS AURELIUS[55]

Identify areas where fear holds you back. What steps
can you take to live more fully?

Coaching Moment

Matteo had always been the dependable one – reliable
at work, present for friends, steady in the family. But
in quieter moments, he'd admit, 'I'm living life on
autopilot.' Every week seemed like a blur of obligations,
and the things he once cared about – painting, hiking,
even quiet evenings with a book – kept getting postponed.

We explored *memento mori*: not in a morbid sense,
but as a reminder of life's fragility.

'If you knew time was running short,' I asked, 'what
would you regret not doing?'

Matteo paused. 'Taking more walks with my dad'
he finally said. 'He's getting older, and I keep saying
"next weekend." I don't want to wait until it's too late.'

The following weekend, Matteo made the call. 'It
wasn't just about the walk,' he shared afterward. 'It was
about waking up to my life again – choosing presence
over postponement.'

---

55   M M Aurelius, *Meditations*, adapted from the public domain
translation by G Long, 1862, Book 12, Section 1.

Week 8
THE ROLE OF REASON AND SELF-DISCIPLINE

'How much more grievous are the consequences of anger than the causes of it.'

– MARCUS AURELIUS[56]

Reflect on moments of anger. How can you manage your emotions to prevent negative outcomes?

Coaching Moment

Riley prided herself on staying composed, but after a tense project review, frustration boiled over. 'I didn't yell,' she admitted, 'but my tone made it clear I was very irritated. I regretted my reaction 10 minutes later.'

Riley reset with a reminder: Always pause before responding, and ask myself, 'Will my response serve the outcome I want?'

Two weeks later, Riley reflected, 'It was humbling. I caught myself snapping at home, too. But that pause helped, and I'm now aware that it is something I need to give greater focus to.'

---

56 M Aurelius, *Meditations*, trans. G Long, 1862, Book 11, Section 18, public domain.

Week 9
PERCEPTION

'The soul becomes dyed with the colour of its thoughts.'

– MARCUS AURELIUS[57]

Consider how your habitual thoughts shape your character. What changes can you make to cultivate a more positive mindset?

Coaching Moment

Jordan, a project lead, often found himself spiralling into negativity after team setbacks. 'It's like one issue triggers a flood of *what ifs* – none of them helpful.'

We discussed how thoughts, like dye, can saturate perspective.

Jordan started a new habit: each time a negative thought surfaced, he'd look to positively reframe it, and ask a question – 'Is this true, or just my fear talking?'

A few weeks in, Jordan noticed a shift. 'I'm not blindly believing my first reaction anymore. I'm asking better questions, and that's making me a steadier, more thoughtful person and leader.'

---

57   M Aurelius, *Meditations*, trans. G Long, 1862, Book 5, Section 16, public domain.

Week 10
FORTITUDE

'Sometimes even to live is an act of courage.'

– SENECA[58]

Acknowledge the challenges you're facing. How can embracing life's difficulties demonstrate your courage?

Coaching Moment

Alex, a senior leader balancing work and personal struggles, shared how he'd been showing up each day feeling emotionally depleted: 'It feels like just getting through the day takes all my energy.'

We reframed the situation through the lens of Stoic courage: 'What if persistence itself is the victory right now?'

Alex embraced that mindset, focusing less on *fixing* everything and more on showing up with integrity, even when things felt hard. 'I stopped judging myself for struggling,' Alex reflected. 'Courage, I realised, is sometimes just continuing to lead when life feels heavy.'

---

58   Seneca, *Moral Letters to Lucilius*, trans. R M Gummere, Loeb Classical Library, Harvard University Press, Cambridge, 1917, Letter 78, public domain.

Week 11
GRIT IN ACTION

'Luck is what happens when preparation meets opportunity.'

– SENECA[59]

Evaluate your goals. How can you prepare now to seize future opportunities?

Coaching Moment

Javier, a senior manager eyeing an executive leadership role, kept postponing preparation. 'I'll get serious when the opportunity comes,' he reasoned.

But what if readiness itself created opportunity?

Javier committed to small, daily actions – building visibility, signalling his interest in next level leadership, and strengthening relationships.

Months later, when an unexpected promotion opened, Javier was the obvious choice. 'It wasn't luck,' he realised. 'It was months of quiet and deliberate preparation finally paying off.'

---

59   This quote is widely attributed to Seneca and reflects ideas from *Moral Letters to Lucilius*, particularly Letter 78, though it does not appear in this exact form in public domain translations.

Week 12
THE FOUR STOIC VIRTUES

He who is brave is free.

– SENECA[60]

What's one small act of bravery that would move things forward this week?

Coaching Moment

Omar hesitated to give constructive feedback to a high-performing member of his team.

'What if it damages the relationship, or demotivates the great work they're producing?' he worried.

We discussed Seneca's point: bravery isn't the absence of fear – it's action despite it.

I asked him to consider, 'What's the greater risk here – a moment of discomfort, or letting the problem quietly grow?'

We also talked about how feedback is part of leadership at every level.

'This is a chance to practise – to build confidence for the next time, and to keep stretching your leadership capacity,' I suggested.

Omar approached the next conversation honestly, focusing on growth rather than blame.

---

60 Commonly attributed to Seneca; reflects ideas from *De Providentia*, Section 2, though not a direct quote.

'It was awkward,' he shared later, 'but liberating. Avoiding hard truths had been weighing me down. Facing it actually strengthened our working relationship. My team member saw I was invested in them and their growth. Feeling fear doesn't have to stop me being brave!'

Week 13
THE ROLE OF REASON AND SELF-DISCIPLINE

'It is the power of the mind to be unconquerable.'

– SENECA[61]

In moments of adversity, how can you strengthen your mind to remain steady?

Coaching Moment

Elena, a team lead managing a difficult stakeholder, often left meetings feeling defeated.

'It's draining,' she shared. 'I can't control their negativity, but it's affecting me.'

We discussed how an *unconquerable mind* means resolve, not control. Elena started each meeting with a mental anchor: *Their behaviour is theirs. My response is mine.*

Elena reflected, 'I can't control the stakeholder, but I can control whether I let them derail my focus.'

---

61   This quote is widely attributed to Seneca and reflects ideas expressed in *De Constantia Sapientis*, Section 5, though it does not appear in this exact form in public domain translations.

Week 14

PERCEPTION

'We suffer more often in imagination than
in reality.'

– SENECA[62]

Identify worries that are based on imagination
rather than fact. How can releasing them reduce
unnecessary stress?

Coaching Moment

Ari often found himself gripped by worry late at night.
'It's like my mind runs wild thinking of everything that
could go wrong tomorrow, next week, next year.'

We discussed Seneca's insight: much of our
suffering comes not from reality, but from the stories
we tell ourselves. Ari agreed to an experiment – each
time a worry arose, he'd write down three lists: What's
actually happening? What am I imagining? And a week
later: What did I learn from this?

At our next check-in, Ari reflected on the impact.
'Ninety percent of my stress was pure imagination. The
real problems were few – and manageable. Writing it
down didn't erase the worry, but it retrained my mind
to pause, question, and respond differently.'

---

62 Seneca, *Moral Letters to Lucilius*, trans. R M Gummere, Loeb
Classical Library, Harvard University Press, Cambridge, 1917, Letter
13, public domain.

The final question – What did I learn from this? – proved the most powerful. 'I started seeing patterns. I realised my worry is often my brain's way of trying to protect me. But when that worry isn't grounded in reality, it's draining. This exercise helped me channel that energy more effectively. Now, instead of spiralling, I ask myself: Is this helpful? What action, if any, do I need to take? If there's nothing to do, I let it go.'

Ari's biggest takeaway? 'I'm managing myself better because I understand my triggers. I can spot the difference between useful caution and pointless rumination. It's not about ignoring worry – it's about making sure it serves me, rather than drains me.'

Week 15
GRATITUDE

'Associate with people who are likely to improve you'.

– SENECA[63]

Assess your professional relationships. Are they fostering your growth and development?

Coaching Moment

Alan, a senior leader, realised his inner circle often defaulted to complaining about work. 'It's hard to stay positive when negativity feels like the norm,' he admitted.

We discussed how relationships shape mindset.

Alan intentionally sought out colleagues who challenged and inspired him.

'It was like switching the air I breathed,' he reflected. 'I feel so much more energised – and this plays out in how I lead.'

---

63   Seneca, *Moral Letters to Lucilius*, trans. R M Gummere, Loeb Classical Library, Harvard University Press, Cambridge, 1917, Letter 7, public domain.

Week 16
GRIT IN ACTION

'Difficulties strengthen the mind, as labour does the body.'

– SENECA[64]

View current challenges as opportunities for mental strengthening. How can this perspective shift your approach?

Coaching Moment

Cheryl was exhausted. 'Every week feels like an uphill climb,' she shared. 'When does it get easier?'

We explored Seneca's idea that difficulty isn't just an obstacle – it's training.

'What if this is hard because it's stretching you in the right ways?' I asked.

Cheryl shifted perspective. Instead of resenting the struggle, she framed each challenge as strength training. 'It didn't make life easier,' she reflected, 'but it made me stronger. I stopped asking, "Why is this happening?" and started asking, "What's this teaching me for next time?"'

---

64   S Seneca, *Moral Letters to Lucilius*, trans. R M Gummere, Loeb Classical Library, Harvard University Press, Cambridge, 1917, Letter 78, public domain.

Week 17
ILLUSION OF CONTROL

'If you wish to escape the things that trouble
you, you need not a change of place, but a
change of self.'

– SENECA[65]

Consider changes you'd like to see in your life. How
can altering your mindset or behaviour bring about
these changes?

Coaching Moment

Morgan, a senior manager, felt frustrated by company
politics.

'I keep thinking, "If only I worked somewhere else,
things would be easier."'

We explored how changing environments often
means carrying the same frustrations with you. Morgan
shifted focus from the external to the internal: *What
can I let go of? What can I influence? And what's actually
within my control?*

Weeks later, Morgan reflected, 'The environment
hasn't changed – but I have. I'm clearer, calmer, and
more deliberate. And these are lessons I'll take with me,
wherever I work next.'

---

65   Seneca, *Moral Letters to Lucilius*, trans. R M Gummere, Loeb
Classical Library, Harvard University Press, Cambridge, 1917, Letter
28, public domain; adapted by the author.

Week 18
GRATITUDE

'Keep hold of your youthful passions – they'll
serve you well when you're older.'

– SENECA[66]

Reconnect with passions from your youth. How can
they enrich your life now?

Coaching Moment

Jenny had always loved music. In her twenties, she'd
lose hours playing guitar – completely absorbed. But
over time, work, family, and responsibility crowded it
out. The guitar sat untouched in the corner.

'It feels silly now,' she said. 'Who has time for
hobbies?'

We talked about Seneca's advice – that reconnecting
with joy isn't indulgent. It's essential.

That week, Jenny picked up the guitar.

'I'm rusty,' she laughed. 'But it's not about sounding
good. It's about remembering who I was before life got
so full.'

Later she reflected, 'That 20-minute break with my
guitar? It clears my head better than anything else. I
thought I didn't have time – but it's what gives me the
energy to handle everything else.'

---

66   Seneca, *Letters from a Stoic*, trans. Richard M. Gummere, Loeb
Classical Library, Heinemann, London, 1917.

Week 19

THE ROLE OF REASON AND SELF-DISCIPLINE

'No man is free who is not master of himself.'

– EPICTETUS[67]

Reflect on areas where you lack self-control. What steps can you take to master yourself?

Coaching Moment

Julia often spoke about feeling 'chained to the screen' – endless scrolling, emails late into the night, Netflix autoplay running until sleep finally won. 'It's like my time isn't my own,' she sighed.

We explored Epictetus' idea that true freedom comes from self-mastery. Julia decided to start small: no phone for the first 30 minutes after waking and the last 30 minutes before bed.

A week later, she shared: 'It felt weird at first, like I was missing something – but I came to realise I wasn't. Instead, I was gaining a window of time!'

'That tiny act of control rippled outward. Once I mastered those bookends of my day, it got easier to reclaim other pockets of time.'

---

67   Epictetus, *Discourses*, trans. E Carter, 1758, Book 3, Chapter 23, public domain.

Week 20
THE FOUR STOIC VIRTUES

'First say to yourself what you would be; and
then do what you have to do.'

– EPICTETUS[68]

Define the person you aspire to be. What actions are
necessary to become that person?

Coaching Moment

Kiran, a leader stepping into a more senior role, shared
a common fear: 'I'm worried I'm not *ready* for this level
of leadership.'

I flipped the question: 'What traits would a
successful leader demonstrate in this role?'

'They'd be clear, calm, and consistent,' Kiran replied.

That's what Kiran practised – steady, deliberate
habits aligned with those traits. The actions came first –
and the confidence grew from there.

---

68   Epictetus, *Discourses*, trans. T W Higginson, 1865, Book 2,
Chapter 10, public domain.

Week 21

ILLUSION OF CONTROL

'Circumstances don't make the man, they only
reveal him to himself.'

– EPICTETUS[69]

In challenging situations, observe what is revealed
about your character. How can this awareness guide
your growth?

Coaching Moment

Jack had always prided himself on being calm
under pressure. But when a close friend cancelled
plans at the last minute – again – he found himself
uncharacteristically upset.

'It's not just the cancellation,' Jack admitted. 'It's
feeling like I don't matter enough for them to follow
through.'

We talked about Epictetus' insight: challenges
reveal our inner state.

'What is this frustration showing you about your
expectations?' I asked.

Jack paused. 'That I tie my sense of worth to how
others treat me,' he realised. 'It's not the cancelled plan
– it's the story I'm telling myself about it.'

---

69   Commonly attributed to Epictetus; reflects ideas from *Discourses*,
Book 1, Chapter 2, though not a direct quote.

With that awareness, the sting softened. Jack decided to speak openly with his friend, not from anger, but from clarity.

'I stopped blaming them for how I felt,' he shared later. 'Instead, I owned my reaction. It strengthened our friendship – and it strengthened my sense of self.'

Week 22
PERCEPTION

'It's not what happens to you, but how you react to it that matters.'

– EPICTETUS[70]

Focus on your reactions to events. How can you choose responses that align with your values?

Coaching Moment

Cath, a project lead, faced sharp criticism after a presentation to her peers didn't go as planned. 'My first instinct was defensiveness – I'd worked so hard on it,' she shared. 'But reacting that way just escalated things, of course, and got us no further with the project.'

What if you focused on what you can control – your response, not your peer's reaction?

Before the next presentation, Cath reminded herself to pause and breathe in response to any harsh feedback. She reminded herself to stay curious, to seek to understand what was beneath the surface of her peer's criticism, to acknowledge her peer's concerns, ask clarifying questions rather than pushing for an outcome.

'This shifted the tone instantly,' Cath reflected. 'Everyone calmed down, and we found a solution faster than I expected.'

---

70 Commonly attributed to Epictetus; reflects ideas from *Discourses* and the *Enchiridion*, especially Section 5, though not a direct quote.

'Turns out,' she smiled, 'slowing down and demonstrating curiosity is a powerful strategic move. As someone who likes to fast track to results, this is quite a revelation for me! This approach works with my kids too!'

Week 23
GRATITUDE

'Only the educated are free.'

– EPICTETUS[71]

Where do you need to invest in your own learning and growth?

Coaching Moment

Kim, a senior leader, felt stuck. 'It's like I've plateaued. I'm just going through the motions.'

I asked what might change if she learned for herself – not just for the role.

Kim committed to 20 minutes of reading each morning – not for work, but for her own growth.

'It surprised me,' she reflected. 'It shifted my energy. It reminded me I'm not done learning – and that opened up a whole new way of thinking.'

---

71   Epictetus, *Discourses*, trans. T W Higginson, 1865, Book 2, Chapter 1, public domain.

Week 24
AMOR FATI

'Seek not the good in external things; seek it in yourselves.'

– EPICTETUS[72]

Reflect on your sources of happiness. Are they dependent on external factors or rooted within you?

Coaching Moment

Jamie had always been someone who thrived on praise. 'When people acknowledge my work, I'm on top of the world. When they don't, I spiral.'

We explored Epictetus' words – true contentment can't rely on external validation.

Jamie decided to try a new approach – after completing any task, he'd pause and ask: 'Did I do my best? Am I proud of how I showed up?'

Two weeks later, he reflected, 'It wasn't easy. I still wanted the gold star. But asking myself those questions shifted the focus inward. I stopped waiting for someone else to tell me I'd done well – and started trusting my own judgment.' Jamie smiled and shared: 'Self-respect feels even better than applause.'

72　Epictetus, *Discourses*, trans. T W Higginson, 1865, Book 1, Chapter 29, public domain.

Week 25

GRATITUDE

'He is a wise man who does not grieve for the things which he has not, but rejoices for those which he has.'

– EPICTETUS[73]

Practice gratitude. What existing aspects of your life can you appreciate more fully – even within your current challenges?

Coaching Moment

Robin had been feeling restless. 'I keep thinking, "Once I get through this tough period, I'll feel better." But the finish line keeps moving.'

We explored Epictetus' reminder: gratitude isn't just about the good times – it's about recognising value in the struggle itself. Robin agreed to try a daily practice: writing down three things she was grateful for within the challenge.

Two weeks later, she reflected, 'It shifted my perspective. I found myself appreciating the grit I was building, the people who supported me, and even the lessons hidden in the hard days. It's not that the challenges disappeared, but gratitude made them feel

---

73   Attributed to Epictetus. While this quote does not appear word-for-word in the surviving texts, it reflects core Stoic themes found in *Discourses* and *Enchiridion*. See also A.A. Long, *Epictetus: A Stoic and Socratic Guide to Life* (Oxford University Press, Oxford, 2002).

less draining – like I was growing through them, not just waiting for them to end.'

Robin's insight? 'I realised it's easy to be grateful when life is smooth. But when you can appreciate what's steadying you during the storm – that's when gratitude really changes things.'

Week 26
MEMENTO MORI

'The whole future lies in uncertainty: live
immediately.'

– SENECA[74]

What's one thing you've been putting off – waiting for
the 'right time' – that you could begin today?

Coaching Moment

Joon, a senior leader, often postponed personal
priorities. 'After this project ends, I'll focus on myself,'
he often said.

We explored how the Stoics used *Memento Mori* –
not to create fear, but to sharpen focus. Time is limited.
Tomorrow isn't guaranteed.

Joon committed to one small, meaningful action
each day – whether it was reaching out to an old friend
or prioritising health.

'It hit me,' Joon reflected. 'I kept waiting for life to
slow down – but life is happening now. *Memento Mori*
isn't morbid – it's a reminder not to postpone what
matters most.'

---

74   Seneca, *Moral Letters to Lucilius*, trans. R M Gummere, Loeb
Classical Library, Harvard University Press, Cambridge, 1917, Letter
101, public domain.

Week 27
THE ROLE OF REASON AND SELF-DISCIPLINE

'Better to trip with the feet than with the tongue.'

– ZENO OF CITIUM[75]

Consider how pausing before speaking might lead to more thoughtful communication this week.

Coaching Moment

Beatriz had always been quick with words – sharp, funny, sometimes biting. 'I don't mean to be harsh,' she admitted, 'but sometimes I speak before I think, and it lands wrong.'

Beatriz decided to practise a simple habit – taking a breath before responding in difficult conversations.

A week later, she shared, 'It felt awkward at first, like I was hesitating too long. But you know what? That pause saved me more than once. I found myself choosing words that actually moved the conversation forward, not sideways.' Beatriz smiled. 'Turns out, silence can be more powerful than the perfect comeback!'

---

75 Attributed to Zeno of Citium; reflects Stoic emphasis on thoughtful speech and self-restraint. See also Diogenes Laertius, *Lives of Eminent Philosophers*, Book 7.

Week 28
PERCEPTION

'Man is affected not by events but by the view he takes of them.'

– EPICTETUS[76]

When faced with difficulty, step back and ask:
How else might I see this situation?

Coaching Moment

Anders was frustrated after receiving critical feedback from a colleague. 'I worked hard on that project, and all they saw were the flaws,' he vented.

We explored Epictetus' insight: could the feedback be viewed not as criticism, but as a blueprint for growth? Anders agreed to reframe the situation, asking: *If I assume the intent was to help, not harm, what changes?*

The following week, he reflected, 'I stopped stewing and started improving. It turns out, the feedback wasn't an attack – it was an opportunity I almost missed because of how I framed it.'

---

76   Commonly attributed to Epictetus; reflects ideas from *Discourses*, Book 1, Chapter 1 and the *Enchiridion*, Section 5, though not a direct quote.

Week 29
AMOR FATI

'Fate leads the willing and drags along the
reluctant.'

– SENECA[77]

How can you embrace the challenges in front of you
rather than resist them?

Coaching Moment

Serj had just been assigned a project he wasn't excited
about. 'It's not where I wanted to focus my energy,'
he sighed.

We explored Seneca's insight: what if embracing the
task – not resisting it – revealed unexpected growth?

Serj reframed the project as an opportunity to
strengthen skills he'd been neglecting. 'I stopped
fighting it and leaned in,' he said later. 'Funnily enough,
the project ended up expanding my leadership visibility,
opening doors I hadn't even considered.'

---

77 Attributed to Seneca; originally from Cleanthes and quoted
approvingly in Seneca's *Moral Letters to Lucilius*, Letter 107.

Week 30
THE FOUR STOIC VIRTUES

'Courage leads to heaven; fear leads to death.'

– SENECA[78]

Where is fear holding you back? What courageous
action can you take this week?

Coaching Moment

Max had been thinking about starting a side project for
years – a blog about their experiences balancing work,
creativity, and well-being. 'But who am I to write about
that?' he often thought. 'What if no one reads it? Or
worse – what if they do, and judge me for it?'

We talked about how fear often masks itself as
waiting for the right time. But Seneca's words struck a
chord: Courage leads to life; fear leads to stagnation.

Max made a decision: he'd write one post, not for
an audience, but for himself. The next week, he shared
the link with a proud smile. 'It's not perfect,' he declared,
'but it's real. And it feels amazing to have done it instead
of just thinking about it.'

---

78   This quote is widely attributed to Seneca and reflects themes from
Moral Letters to Lucilius, though it does not appear verbatim in public
domain translations..

Week 31
GRATITUDE

'Gratitude is not only the greatest of virtues but
the parent of all others.'

– CICERO[79]

What can you appreciate more fully today, both in
yourself and those around you?

Coaching Moment

Laura, feeling disconnected from her team, realised
most conversations were task-driven. 'I'm so focused
on outcomes, I forget the people behind them,'
she shared.

We explored how practising gratitude – expressing
appreciation for effort and connection, not just results
– might shift dynamics.

'It was almost instant,' Laura later reflected. 'When
I started noticing what my team was getting right –
not just where we fell short – morale lifted, and so did
collaboration.'

---

79   Cicero, *Pro Plancio*, 54 BCE, Section 82, public domain.

Week 32

ILLUSION OF CONTROL

'The wise man looks for everything from
himself; the ignorant man expects everything
from others.'

– EPICTETUS[80]

How could focusing on what's within your control
change your leadership this week?

Coaching Moment

Simone was frustrated with a direct report who kept
missing deadlines. 'I've explained expectations so many
times – why isn't it clicking?'

What if you focused less on their behaviour and
more on how you set them up for success?

Simone clarified expectations, organised regular
check-ins, and asked, 'What support do you need from
me to make this happen?'

'It didn't just improve their performance,' Simone
reflected. 'It reminded me that leadership isn't
about controlling others – it's about offering clarity
and accountability, and ensuring that this is built
on a foundation of trust and connection. I need to
demonstrate I've got their back, before I critique results.'

---

80   This quote is widely attributed to Epictetus and reflects themes
from *Enchiridion*, Section 5, though it does not appear in this exact
form in public domain translations.

Week 33
GRIT IN ACTION

'Do not pray for an easy life; pray for the strength to endure a difficult one.'

– BRUCE LEE[81]

What challenge can you face head-on this week with greater inner resolve?

Coaching Moment

Arjun was navigating a difficult team transition after a colleague's sudden departure. 'Everyone's stressed, and I'm supposed to hold it together,' he admitted.

What if the strength needed isn't about suppressing your stress, but acknowledging it, appropriately, while moving forward?

Arjun chose transparency – acknowledging the strain while reinforcing the team's strengths. 'It didn't solve the workload overnight,' he reflected, 'but it built trust. People appreciated that I didn't pretend everything was fine – I led through it, not around it.'

He came to realise that this period had given him an opportunity to develop greater inner resolve: 'Now, when life throws curveballs, I don't wait for ease – I focus on showing up, and then look for the lessons from there.'

---

81   This quote is widely attributed to Bruce Lee, though no verified source in his published writings confirms this exact phrasing.

Week 34

THE ROLE OF REASON AND SELF-DISCIPLINE

'No man is more unhappy than he who never
faces adversity. For he is not permitted to
prove himself.'

– SENECA[82]

Consider your current challenges. How might they be
shaping you into a stronger leader?

Coaching Moment

Remy was overwhelmed after stepping into an interim
leadership role. 'I'm in over my head,' he admitted.

We explored Seneca's wisdom: 'Can you reframe
this as an opportunity to develop your leadership?'
I asked.

Remy leaned into the discomfort, focusing on
learning rather than perfection.

'It's still hard,' he shared later, 'but I'm less afraid
of mistakes. I realised leadership isn't about always
knowing the answer – it's about staying steady when
you don't.'

---

82   Widely attributed to Seneca, this quote reflects key themes from
De Providentia and *Moral Letters to Lucilius*, particularly Letters 67
and 78.

Week 35

THE FOUR STOIC VIRTUES

'Do not explain your philosophy. Embody it.'

– EPICTETUS[83]

In what area of your life can you demonstrate your values rather than just speak about them?

Coaching Moment

Nisha often spoke about the importance of balance – making time for family, health, and personal growth. Yet, her calendar told a different story: back-to-back meetings, late nights, weekends swallowed by work.

'I talk about balance,' Nisha admitted, 'but I'm not living it.'

We explored Epictetus' challenge: *What would it look like to embody balance, not just value it?*

Nisha started small – blocking time for morning walks and keeping one evening a week phone-free.

'At first, it felt indulgent,' she reflected. 'But then I realised: I wasn't just protecting my time. I was aligning my life with my values. And that felt more genuine than any speech about balance ever could.'

---

83   Commonly attributed to Epictetus; reflects themes from *Discourses*, Book 1, Chapter 4.

Week 36
FORTITUDE

'The greater the difficulty, the more glory in
overcoming it.'

– EPICTETUS[84]

What challenge can you tackle with fortitude this week?

Coaching Moment

Lauren was managing a tough reorganisation at work
while feeling on the cusp of burnout. 'It's hard to lead
when you're running on empty,' she admitted.

We discussed Epictetus' perspective. I asked,
'Can you reframe this difficulty as an opportunity to
strengthen you, rather than deplete you? What small
changes can you make in response.'

Lauren focused on small, consistent actions –
checking in with her team, practising self-care, and
keeping communication clear.

'The reorganisation didn't get easier,' she shared,
'but the reframe stopped me feeling powerless. I know
grit is not about perfection – it's about persistence, one
decision at a time. And that is within my control.'

'And alongside that, fortitude means sometimes it's
ok to stand still in the storm – I don't always need to
keep pushing.'

---

84   Widely attributed to Epictetus; reflects themes from *Discourses*,
Book 1, Chapter 24.

Week 37
PERCEPTION

'Build your life action by action. Be content if each one is done with purpose and integrity – no one can stop you from this.'

– MARCUS AURELIUS[85]

Are you measuring your leadership by results you can't control – or by the actions you can take today?

Coaching Moment

Casey, a senior leader managing an underperforming team, was exhausted.

'I'm tired of fixing the same issues,' she said. 'It feels like nothing's changing.'

Instead of trying to overhaul everything at once, we explored a mindset shift: what if progress didn't have to mean fixing the whole thing immediately? What if the real shift came from how she saw the situation – and how she chose to respond, one step at a time?

That landed.

'The team didn't suddenly become high-performing,' Casey reflected, 'but I did change how I approached it. I stopped focusing on what wasn't working and started focusing on what I could influence that day. A conversation. A clear expectation. A moment of positive reinforcement.'

---

85   M Aurelius, *Meditations*, adapted from the public domain translation by G Long, 1862, Book 8, Section 32.

That shift in perspective gave her back a sense of control – and slowly, the team began to shift too.

Build your life action by action. That's what Casey did.

Week 38
MEMENTO MORI

'You could leave this life at any moment. Let that awareness shape what you do, say, and think.'

– MARCUS AURELIUS[86]

How might this perspective influence your choices today?

Coaching Moment

Jill had been meaning to call an old friend for months. 'I'll do it when things slow down,' she kept saying. But things never slowed down.

One evening, after a particularly long day, Jill saw the quote on her desk: 'You could leave life right now.' She picked up the phone and dialled.

'We talked for an hour,' Jill shared the next week. 'Nothing dramatic, just catching up. But I came to realise I'd been putting off much-needed connection for no good reason.'

Jill smiled. 'When you remember life's fragility, you stop waiting for *later* and start choosing *now*.'

---

86   Adapted from Marcus Aurelius, *Meditations*, Book 2, Section 11, public domain translations including G Long (1862).

Week 39

GRATITUDE

'Enjoy present pleasures in such a way as not to
injure future ones.'

– SENECA[87]

Where might practicing moderation improve both your
present and future?

Coaching Moment

Ryan, balancing a demanding role and family life, often
sacrificed sleep to catch up on work. 'I'll rest when
things calm down,' he said.

We discussed how moderation protects future well-
being. Ryan committed to a firm evening cut-off time.

'It felt counterintuitive, and it took self-discipline,'
he reflected, 'but I became more effective during the
day – and more present at home. Moderation protected
what mattered most.'

---

87   Seneca, *Moral Letters to Lucilius*, trans. R M Gummere, Loeb
Classical Library, Harvard University Press, Cambridge, 1917, Letter
19, public domain.

Week 40
ILLUSION OF CONTROL

'Freedom is the only worthy goal in life. It is won by disregarding things that lie beyond our control.'

– EPICTETUS[88]

What worries can you set aside by focusing only on what you can control?

Coaching Moment

Avery, leading a high-stakes project, was overwhelmed by external dependencies.

'I'm constantly chasing updates I can't control,' she shared.

Instead, we shifted attention inward: What's fully within your control?

Avery doubled down on team readiness and clear communication.

'Once I let go of chasing certainty,' she reflected, 'I found peace in focusing on what I could actually influence.'

---

88   Widely attributed to Epictetus; reflects themes from *Discourses*, 1.29, and *Enchiridion*, 1

Week 41
THE ROLE OF REASON AND SELF-DISCIPLINE

'Speech in haste is unguarded speech.'

– SENECA[89]

Where might slowing down your words create better outcomes this week?

Coaching Moment

Leo, frustrated by a colleague's criticism, was ready to send a pointed follow-up email.

We talked about how quick reactions rarely lead to good outcomes – and are often the ones you regret.

Leo waited. The next day, he responded calmly and clearly.

Later he reflected, 'I was glad I didn't send that first reply. It wouldn't have helped – and it's not how I want to lead.'

---

89 Widely attributed to Seneca; reflects themes from *Moral Letters to Lucilius*, especially Letters 88, 94, and 114.

Week 42
AMOR FATI

'Misfortune is virtue's opportunity.'

– SENECA[90]

When you look back on a current challenge, what do you hope your actions will show about your character?

Coaching Moment

Michelle was passed over for a promotion she'd worked hard for. 'It's hard not to take it personally,' she admitted.

We discussed Seneca's insight: what if the disappointment is actually a proving ground for your values of strength and poise?

Michelle chose to congratulate the colleague who got the role, while asking for feedback to guide future growth.

'It wasn't easy,' she shared, 'but how I handled that moment defined me far more than the promotion itself. And ironically, staying grounded boosted my credibility as a leader.'

This experience extended Michelle's perspective more broadly. 'I stopped seeing setbacks as *failure* and started seeing them as character-building moments.'

---

90   Widely attributed to Seneca; reflects themes from *De Providentia*, especially Section 4.

Week 43

THE FOUR STOIC VIRTUES

'Virtue is nothing else than right reason.'

– SENECA[91]

What helps you stay anchored in clear thinking when
the pressure is on?

Coaching Moment

Evan was torn about whether to accept a promotion
that would mean more hours but exciting work. 'Do I
choose ambition or balance?'

We explored Seneca's view: what if the 'right'
decision isn't about ambition or sacrifice – but
alignment with your values?

Evan reflected on what mattered most – autonomy,
impact, and well-being.

'I turned down the promotion,' he shared later, 'but
negotiated a role expansion that honoured both my
career goals and personal priorities.'

---

91   Seneca, *Moral Letters to Lucilius*, trans. R M Gummere, Loeb
Classical Library, Harvard University Press, Cambridge, 1917, Letter
66, public domain.

Week 44
FORTITUDE

'The greater the obstacle, the more glory in overcoming it.'

– MOLIÈRE[92]

What obstacle can you approach with renewed determination this week?

Coaching Moment

Jordan, an executive stepping into a new role, quickly encountered resistance. 'I thought getting the promotion would be the hard part,' he admitted. 'But now, it feels like every decision is challenged.'

We explored fortitude: what if resistance isn't a sign you're off track, but proof you're in the middle of the work that matters?

Jordan shifted his approach. Instead of reacting to pushback, he focused on steady, consistent leadership. 'It's still hard,' Jordan reflected, 'but I'm not burning energy fighting the challenge. I'm working through it, one conversation at a time.'

---

92   Moli Molière, *The School for Wives* (1662). Cited here for its Stoic-aligned view on adversity, though Molière was a 17th-century French playwright, not a Stoic philosopher.

Week 45

GRATITUDE

'Do not spoil what you have by desiring what you have not.'

– EPICURUS[93]

What blessings are you overlooking because you're focused on what's missing?

Coaching Moment

Gary had always been ambitious – setting goals, hitting them, and quickly moving on to the next. 'I should be happy,' he confessed, 'but it feels like I'm always chasing something just out of reach.'

We talked about Epicurus' reminder: gratitude anchors us in the present. Gary agreed to try something simple – ending each day by naming three things he already had and valued.

A month later, he reflected, 'Such a simple daily practice changed how I saw my life. Instead of focusing on what I didn't have, I started noticing what was already good – my health, my friendships, even just the quiet moments in between tasks.'

'And the funny thing?' Gary added. 'Once I appreciated what I had, I didn't stop striving. But I stopped feeling like happiness was always one achievement away. My mood lightened, and my energy rose.'

---

93   Epicurus, *Letter to Menoeceus*, in *The Extant Remains*, trans. C D Yonge, 1853, public domain. Greek philosopher (not a Stoic), known for his insights on happiness, moderation, and the pursuit of a simple life.

Week 46

GRIT IN ACTION

'Courage doesn't always roar. Sometimes
courage is the quiet voice at the end of the day
saying, "I will try again tomorrow."'

– MARY ANNE RADMACHER[94]

Where can you apply more patience and persistence in
your leadership?

Coaching Moment

Priya, an experienced executive, was leading a major
organisational change. Progress was slow. Setbacks
kept coming.

'I'm used to working hard,' she said. 'But this feels
different. It's not about doing more – it's about staying
with it.'

We talked about grit as staying power – not forcing
outcomes, but showing up, day after day, for what
matters most.

Months later, when the change finally began to take
hold, Priya reflected:

'It wasn't one big moment that made the difference.
It was showing up on the days I didn't feel like it. That's
what got us there.'

---

94   M A Radmacher, *Courage Doesn't Always Roar*, Conari Press, San
Francisco, 2009.

Week 47
PERCEPTION

'The mind that is anxious about future events is miserable.'

– SENECA[95]

What future concern can you set aside to focus fully on the present?

Coaching Moment

Kylie, anticipating leadership changes, felt on edge.

'I keep thinking, "What if the new structure doesn't favour my team?"'

We discussed how future anxiety steals present peace. Kylie committed to focusing only on current priorities.

'Letting go of *what ifs*,' she reflected, 'gave me back energy for what actually mattered. The future will come – but I'm leading in the now.'

---

95 Seneca, *Moral Letters to Lucilius*, trans. R M Gummere, Loeb Classical Library, Harvard University Press, Cambridge, 1917, Letter 98, public domain.

Week 48
THE FOUR STOIC VIRTUES

'Wisdom begins in wonder.'

– SOCRATES[96]

What question can you explore more deeply this week
to expand your understanding?

Coaching Moment

Blake, preparing for a strategic pivot, felt stuck. 'I don't
have all the answers,' he admitted.

We explored the power of inquiry. Instead of forcing
solutions, Blake leaned into questions: What haven't we
considered? What assumptions are we making?

'It opened new doors,' he shared. 'Curiosity led to
insights that certainty never could.'

---

96   Widely attributed to Socrates; reflects his teaching as recorded
in Plato's *Theaetetus*, 155d. Ancient Greek philosopher who deeply
influenced Stoic thought, especially through Plato's dialogues.

Week 49
FORTITUDE

'What stands in the way becomes the way.'

– MARCUS AURELIUS[97]

What obstacle can you transform into an opportunity this week?

Coaching Moment

David, facing budget cuts, worried about derailed initiatives. 'This will set us back,' he said.

We explored the Stoic approach: What if the constraint drives innovation?

David rallied the team around creative solutions. 'The obstacle forced focus,' he reflected. 'We ended up with leaner, sharper projects.'

---

97   M Aurelius, *Meditations*, adapted from the public domain translation by G Long, 1862, Book 5, Section 20.

Week 50
THE ROLE OF REASON AND SELF-DISCIPLINE

'To bear trials with a calm mind robs misfortune of its strength and burden.'

– SENECA[98]

How can you approach a current difficulty with greater calm and clarity?

Coaching Moment

Amy, juggling multiple priorities, felt overwhelmed. 'Everything feels urgent,' she remarked.

She practised slowing things down – taking a moment to ask, What's essential? What's noise?

It didn't change the workload – but it changed her response. She didn't have to do everything at once. She just needed to focus on the next step.

---

98   Widely attributed to Seneca; reflects themes from *De Providentia* and *Moral Letters to Lucilius*, particularly Letters 78 and 104 (public domain).

Week 51
AMOR FATI

'If a man knows not to which port he sails, no
wind is favourable.'

– SENECA[99]

Clarify your objectives. Are your daily actions and
habits aligned with your ultimate goals?

Coaching Moment

Stefan, a senior leader, was feeling burnt out. 'I'm always
busy, but I'm not sure I'm moving toward anything
meaningful.'

We explored Seneca's metaphor: if you don't know
your destination, how can you navigate effectively?

Stefan clarified his personal and professional
priorities: 'I want to lead with impact, but not at the
cost of my health or relationships.'

This clarity reshaped everything. They set tighter
boundaries, articulated their non-negotiables, prioritised
strategic focus areas, and encouraged their team to do
the same.

Stefan reflected, 'Once I knew my *port*, it became
easier to say no to distractions – and yes to what
truly matters.'

99   L. A. Seneca, *Letters to Lucilius*, trans. R.M. Gummere, Loeb
Classical Library, Harvard University Press, Cambridge MA, 1917.
Public domain

Week 52

MEMENTO MORI

*'Live as if you were living for the second time
and had acted wrongly the first time.'*

– VIKTOR FRANKL[100]

What would you do differently if you treated today as a second chance?

Coaching Moment

Nathan, reflecting on a year of missed personal priorities, sighed. 'Work took over. Again.'

We explored the *memento mori* mindset: If today were your do-over, what would you prioritise?

Nathan restructured his calendar – protecting time for family and health. 'I stopped waiting for balance to *happen* and made it a key focus each and every day.'

---

100   V E Frankl, *Man's Search for Meaning*, Beacon Press, Boston, 2006.

These 52 reflections offer a moment of pause each week – a chance to check in with yourself, recalibrate, and stay on track. It's not just the big decisions that shape how we lead and live – it's the quiet, everyday choices we make. How we respond to pressure. How we treat others. How we stay true to what matters.

Marcus Aurelius didn't write Meditations for an audience. He wrote it for himself – a way to reflect, stay grounded, and hold himself to the standards he believed in.

I hope these reflections do the same for you.

Conclusion

THE ONGOING PRACTICE OF ANCHORED AND INTENTIONAL LEADERSHIP

So here we are.

You've explored what it means to be anchored – to manage your mindset, let go of control, and navigate uncertainty without letting it destabilise you. To shift your perception, focus on what's within your power, and meet challenges with acceptance rather than resistance. To think clearly, regulate emotion, and respond with reason rather than reaction.

You've explored what it means to be intentional – to take action in alignment with what matters, to move forward with purpose, and to stay in motion even when things get hard. To practise grit. To stay with the work for the long haul.

And you've seen how fortitude is the last card we all hold – when action isn't enough, when effort isn't working, and when all that's left is the choice to accept and endure.

Now, the invitation is yours.

Because leadership doesn't happen in perfect conditions. It's not something you practise in theory. It's shaped in the real moments – when things go wrong, when you feel stuck, when you're asked to make a decision with no guarantee of the outcome.

Maybe you'll be pushing toward a goal – but progress is slow.

Maybe you'll be leading a team through uncertainty – and resistance shows up where you didn't expect it.

Maybe, despite your best efforts, a key project goes off track.

Or maybe everything is going well. The work is flowing. The team is in rhythm. Progress feels good.

Even then – especially then – the invitation is the same.

Be grounded. Be deliberate.

Step back. Reflect. Apply what you've cultivated.

A way of steadying yourself.

A way of thinking clearly.

A way of staying true to what matters most – and taking the next step.

Showing up, again and again, with clarity, grit, and the willingness to keep going.

Stay Anchored. Be Intentional.